on campus cookbook

by mollie fitzgerald

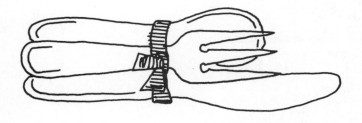

illustrations by l.k. hanson

workman publishing new york

Copyright © 1984 by Mollie Jean Fitzgerald

Library of Congress Cataloging in Publication Data

Fitzgerald, Mollie.
    On campus cookbook.

    Includes index.
    1. Cookery.   I. Title.
TX652.F526   1984   641.5   84-40319
ISBN 0-89480-775-7

Art director: Paul Hanson
Book design: Susan Aronson Stirling
Cover and book illustrator: L. K. Hanson

Workman Publishing Company, Inc.
1 West 39 Street
New York, NY 10018

Manufactured in the United States of America
First printing August 1984
10 9 8 7 6 5 4 3 2 1

dedication

This book is dedicated to my mother, Susan Fitzgerald, for her creative brainstorms and insights, perpetual and contagious optimism, patience and assistance both in and out of the kitchen—and her love, without which I would never have embarked upon such a project.

acknowledgments

Writing a book while still in college has been a demanding but invaluable experience. It's as if I've been taking an extra course each semester, with my spring breaks highlighted by manuscript revisions after my summers have been spent at the typewriter.

So many people have been so kind in helping me pull this book together: from those who cultivated my gourmet cooking skills, offered recipes, taste-tested, read, critiqued, typed and retyped my earliest drafts (which were rough, at best) to those who headed up the camera crews for my cable TV cooking show at Duke. To each and every one of you for adding your own special ingredient, I am most appreciative.

It is appropriate here, however, to recognize a few individuals for whose integral contributions I am most grateful:

My grandmother, Marjorie Asbury, for developing a rich and long-standing tradition of good cooking in our family, and who knew long ago that I would someday write a cookbook.

My confidante, Mike Harrington, for her enthusiasm which sustained me in the early phases, and for her reconnaissance efforts and assistance with details which allowed me to pursue my studies at Duke.

Duke University for providing me the unique opportunity to create and produce my own cooking show on television, which in turn prompted me to write this book.

My editor, Suzanne Rafer, for her confidence and support in my ideas; my copy editor, Kathie Ness, for helping to fine tune my recipes; and Workman Publishing for making a dream come true.

My Duke roommates and dearest friends, Vicky Hart, Audrey Grumhaus, Nancy Davis, and Libby Sunderland, who supported me a hundred percent of the way as they watched their dorm room turn into a kitchen of sprawling proportions (as well as a television studio); who happily ate the flops as well as the successes; and in whom I'm determined to one day spawn an interest in cooking.

The idea of dorm-room cooking was born on a snowy drive from Duke to my home in Pittsburgh, and my deepest thanks go to my friend Walter Deane for his creative and persistent encouragement in helping me develop and promote the concept of dorm-room cooking.

contents

non-kitchen cooking

talk to anyone on campus and the most widespread complaint you'll hear is about the food. Many students dread mealtimes—the lines, the noise, the limited hours, and especially the food itself. One solution seems to be snacking on candy bars, pizza, and potato chips, washed down with Coke or coffee. Admittedly we keep erratic hours at college—nothing is going to change that—but the erratic eating habits have got to go! Not only are these snacks packed with calories (remember, freshmen aren't the only ones who can gain that "freshman fifteen") but they also don't satisfy your hunger. The result: you eat too much.

And on top of that, what you're eating isn't nutritious.

It's no use blaming the university food services. The cafeteria is usually doing the best it can. Running a kitchen of those dimensions is no easy task. Remember, they're feeding thousands of people, with budgetary constraints and government dietary requirements to meet. What you need is a workable, easy alternative for an occasional break from the cafeteria routine.

Maybe you'd like to get away from all that starchy food. Or you'd like to satisfy a certain craving that the cafeteria menus just don't meet. Or you'd like to entertain (and impress) your date or a few friends. Perhaps you want to take a picnic to a park or beach that's not just deli stuff? Or just because you're hungry and don't feel like going to the cafeteria (it's raining, you're not feeling social, or it's 3:00 A.M. and everything is closed), you'd like to be able to fix something to snack on. Whatever your reasons, this book gives you recipes, helpful hints, and serving suggestions—all guaranteed to make cooking and entertaining in your dormitory room a fun event.

Preparing food in your dorm might not be exactly "legal" at all colleges. Often the fire code will prohibit certain cooking activities, and in older buildings the electrical wiring may not tolerate the addition of even minor appliances in your room. Get the specifics. Speak to the authorities. Many times it's hot plates or electric frying pans that are prohibited, not hot pots, toaster ovens, and blenders, which are the only cooking appliances used in this book. Also, many dorms and sorority/fraternity houses have kitchens (some even have one on each floor) available for student use. If this is the case, you're lucky, for that opens up a whole new realm of cooking possibilities. So if you would like to cook every so often, be sure to investigate all the avenues. No matter where you end up doing the actual cooking, this book will help. At the same time, I do urge caution. Don't go against school policy just to enjoy a snack or indulge in a little dormitory cuisine.

Few students really know how to cook. Most of them are "afraid." If you are scared to try a recipe, you have probably successfully avoided the kitchen at home for years, at least until it was cleanup time. Maybe you were lucky enough to have had a "supermom" to coordinate and cook all your meals. This cookbook is meant to help the novice overcome fear, develop confidence, and actually enjoy concocting and creating good (good for you and good to eat) food. *Cooking really is fun!*

Besides fulfilling a basic need of life—sustenance— cooking is unique because it can also be a hobby and a creative art form. Face it, laundry, vacuuming, and other "life support systems" do not lend themselves to this kind of inspiration. Furthermore, it is very gratifying to bring people together to share a meal, particularly one you've made yourself. Creative cooking can be habit-forming, thus making it an enjoyable task for the rest of your life. Even some of the simplified tips and techniques you learn in this book, which are the bare essentials, can be expanded and used in many ways for years to come. So consider this to be one of your more practical textbooks as you start out on campus.

On the other hand, if you've always had an interest in cooking, the transition from a well-equipped kitchen at home to a dorm room with limited space and few appliances is a different kind of challenge. After many frustrating moments, I have refined procedures down to an easy system. My interpretations of home-cooked meals with the "à la campus" touch are quick, inexpensive, and satisfying. What more could you ask for?

These recipes are prepared with one or more of three common appliances: a *hot pot,* a *toaster oven,* and a *blender.* These are generally on the approved list of the housing departments of most universities. If you really get hooked, enjoy experimenting, and want to expand, I would recommend an electric wok as the next step. This will open up lots of new options, especially for meats and vegetables. But for now, let's stick with the basics.

The quick and easy recipes here have all been adapted to fit your college lifestyle. No matter how keen your interest in cooking, no student has hours to "slave over the open fire" or to clean up after an extravagant meal. I've kept things simple on purpose. Even if your dorm room can be very functional as a kitchen, it also happens to be your bedroom, study, and (now with this book) your dining room. And don't forget about your roommate, who may not be as enthusiastic about cooking in the room as you are. So be sure to get his or her go-ahead before you start. Maybe your roommate will also enjoy cooking, or better yet, doesn't mind cleaning up. Yes, those people really do exist: anything for real food!

I have also tried to anticipate any problems you might have along the way, like shopping, how to store equipment, tips for hassle-free cleanup, possible substitutions if you can't find or afford one of the ingredients.

As I prepare a recipe in my dorm room, I always ask myself, could this be done in an easier way? How important is this step or this ingredient? Could I substitute this for that? Once you develop a little expertise in your own dorm-room kitchen, I encourage you to ask yourself these same questions and adapt some of your favorite family recipes to your facilities. I have also asked some of my friends at colleges and universities all over the country to submit some of their suggestions for quick dormitory meals, and they are included here with my own recipes.

One more thing, and this is addressed to the men: cooking is not just for women! Some of the most enthusiastic cooks I've met are men. Your date will be impressed when you invite her over for hors d'oeuvres before the next dance, and so will your study-group friends when you fortify them with great-tasting midnight snacks. Go ahead, give it a try!

setting up chez dorm

here is a list of ideas to make your life as a campus cook a little easier—things to keep in mind when setting up your "kitchen." Just because you want to cook doesn't mean you want to spend a lot of money. College students are very resourceful, and the three I's—imagination, improvisation, and ingenuity—come in handy here.

• **Save all aluminum foil pans.** Many things, especially frozen foods, come in foil pans. Sara Lee and Pepperidge Farm goodies are ideal sources. Don't throw them away; these pans are great because they're small enough to fit in the toaster oven and in the tiny refrigerators in dorm rooms. And the best part of it all is that

you can dispose of them after use—so no cleanup. On the outside chance that you are not a Sara Lee addict, these pans are available inexpensively and in every shape and size in most supermarkets.

• **Save all plastic containers.** These are super for storing leftovers in the fridge. Lots of things come in plastic containers, such as yogurt, margarine, cottage cheese, chicken salad from your last store-bought picnic.

Do *not* invest in expensive pots, knives, or bowls since they have a mysterious way of disappearing. Plastic knives, forks, and spoons, as well as paper plates, cups, and napkins are super for dorm room use. Anyway, it's really great to be able to throw things away if the going gets messy. And who has the space for a collection of pots and pans?

• **Buy your ingredients in small quantities.** Disregard the rule of buying in large quantity to minimize cost. The dorm room is one place where that won't work. At college you're up against problems not encountered at home: Where to store all those giant "family-size" packages? Many items have a limited

shelf life and you will never be able to use up large amounts before they spoil. Most important, you want to avoid keeping a lot of open food around which will attract unwelcome creatures like ants, mice, or cockroaches! You'll be saving yourself money in the long run by not having to throw anything away.

• **Take advantage of "doggie bags."** Don't be embarrassed about the service many restaurants offer—wrapping up the remainder of a large portion you couldn't finish for you to take home. Combined with other ingredients, it can be a delicious feature for a sandwich or soup the next day. Also remember to save any extra ketchup, mustard, and other condiment packets you get with a fast-food meal. These, and sugar packets, always come in handy.

• **Keep paper towels on hand at all times.** They have multiple uses: for spills, drying dishes, or as napkins for a casual affair. It's easy to make a paper towel dispenser, too: Pound two nails into the wall about 14 inches apart. String a piece of twine through the roll and tie a knot at each end, slipping the knot over each nail. Or maybe a grateful guest will present you with the real thing!

• **Store things in tiered hanging baskets** made of wire mesh, available in most cooking shops and department stores. These are great because you can stash napkins, spices, utensils, food, or just about anything that you would like to get up out of the way. The advantage with the wire mesh is that you can see what's inside. Another tip is to mount a clothesline (the same way you did the paper towel holder) and use clothespins or hooks to hang hot pads, dish towels, a scrub brush, an apron, etc. To avoid having everything slide together in the middle, tie big knots at intervals along the line.

• **Take this cookbook to the grocery store with you** so you'll be sure to remember the ingredients and the quantities. This will keep you from having to return for forgotten items and from giving in to whims and buying things that look good but aren't practical. Of course, you can always make a list instead of bringing the book along.

how to choose your appliance

This is by no means a complete list of gadgets you can buy for your dorm-room kitchen, nor is it a brand selection guide; but because all of the recipes in this book are based upon the use of the hot pot, toaster oven, blender, and refrigerator, I cannot emphasize enough the importance of selecting the right models. Since most of you are probably first-time appliance buyers, I've provided some basic guidelines so that you may approach this potentially overwhelming situation objectively and with confidence.

Perhaps a few of you will be lucky enough to have an extra, retired toaster oven or blender at home, which you can resurrect from the basement. Otherwise, the first rule of thumb is to go to a store large enough to have a big selection. Analyze the different sizes, options, and models relative to their price. Allow yourself plenty of time to make your decision and be sure to read the labels carefully. Keep your purchase simple: many of the fancy options are expensive and unnecessary for dorm-room cooking.

If you're coming to college as a freshman, perhaps you'll want to contact your future roommate in advance to see who's bringing what and to avoid duplications. If you're returning as an upperclassman, also consult your cooking buddies before buying any of these appliances so that you can share the cost of the investment.

Hot Pot. This is perhaps the most useful (and inexpensive—around $20) of the dorm-room appliances. Don't confuse it with a crock pot, hot shot, or hot plate.

Look for a hot pot with a 6-cup capacity, as this will best suit your dorm-room needs. Teflon coating on the inside is a convenient option, but not necessary.

Blender. When choosing a blender, you may be confronted with an entire wall of possibilities; I suggest you select one that is medium-priced, around $25 to $30. You certainly don't need the top-of-the-line model, although you should choose one with more than two controls—in other words, more than just on/off. Make sure your selection has a plastic work bowl; a plastic one is much lighter and easier to work with than glass, and it won't break if it is accidentally dropped. Remember, it has to last you at least four years!

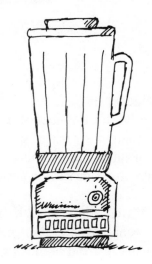

Toaster Oven. Like stereos, video tape recorders, and food processors, the state-of-the-art toaster oven is constantly reaching new pinnacles. Stay away from models with new-fangled touches (the ones that look more like miniature microwave ovens). These options are completely unnecessary for the dorm-room setup and will cost you dearly. Besides, who needs a self-cleaning toaster oven?

Look for a toaster oven in the $35 to $50 range with a broil, toast, and bake combination. Check for a thermostat so that you'll be able to set it at a specific temperature. There are several brands and models that fall into this no-nonsense category, and any of these will serve you well in your college cooking career. (Of all the appliances, this one will probably show the most wear and tear—grease and grime—at the end of your four years.)

Refrigerator. Before embarking on your dorm-room cooking career, locate the nearest available refrigerator—it might be a large community fridge shared by the dorm hall, or one owned by your next-door neighbor. Some of these recipes require a refrigerator, and having access to one will make things easier all around.

If you're interested in buying your own miniature fridge for your room (though this is not necessary), there are many shapes, sizes, and brands from which to choose. If you don't want to invest in a new one, you can usually buy one very reasonably from an upperclassman who is graduating or moving to an apartment. Look for a refrigerator with a freezer compartment large enough for a few miniature ice trays.

essentials for your dorm-room kitchen

Utensils.

2 sharp knives—1 paring knife and 1 medium size

1 wooden spoon

1 rubber spatula

1 wire whisk

1 hand grater

1 small cutting board

1 tray or large plate (for serving and as an extra work surface)

2 bowls—1 large and 1 small

Aluminum foil

Wax paper

Paper towels

Paper plates

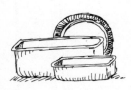

Aluminum foil pans (see page 12)

Plastic bags—medium size

Food Staples.

You probably won't want to stock up on these all at once, but here are the basics that will let you be better prepared for that spur-of-the-moment occasion.

Salt and pepper

"Nature's Seasons," a nice combo of
    herbs and salt, or your favorite
    seasoned salt

Dried parsley flakes

Mixed Italian herbs

Basil (my favorite herb)

Onion powder—to substitute for the
    real thing

Garlic salt or powder

Chicken and beef bouillon cubes

Ground cinnamon

Bisquick, in a box or premeasured
    individual packets

Small bags (2 pounds) sugar and all-
    purpose flour

Alfalfa sprouts

Chives and parsley plants—also easy to
    grow from a hanging basket or on a
    windowsill

Crackers—Wheat Thins and others, great for snacks or if you're out of bread

Peanut butter and jelly—probably two staples you have already!

Toothpicks

Bottles of white wine and beer, if allowed—not only for drinking, but also to use in some recipes

Refrigerator items.

Butter or margarine

Small jar mayonnaise

Plain yogurt

Sour cream

Cream cheese

Heavy or whipping cream

Cheez Whiz

Parmesan cheese

Lemons or lemon juice

Specialty Items.

These are for special occasions and will really jazz up your menu.

Sherry if allowed—an inexpensive dry sherry to spike sauces. Cooking sherry, which is available in grocery stores, is fine for cooking, not for drinking.

Chutney—a tangy relish sauce great for cold meats and open-face sandwiches.

Pommery mustard (or other unusual variety in an attractive jar) for salads and sandwiches.

Tabasco sauce—self-explanatory!

Jars of crab and/or baby shrimp. Very versatile: add to soups and salads; serve with cream cheese and crackers for hors d'oeuvres; mix with mayonnaise for a super picnic sandwich; or eat them straight out of the jar.

Pickles, olives, and relishes—if you like these, look for unique kinds, the more exotic the better! Serve them with absolutely anything that strikes your fancy.

Pepperidge Farm cookies—These seem to go well with anything! The Pirouettes are especially elegant—serve on doilies, of course—and the chocolate ones are irresistible!

Smoked oysters or smoked clams—both come in tiny cans. The right person will really appreciate these . . . and oysters are rumored to be an effective aphrodisiac (as are parsley stems)! So save them for the right occasion.

"Party" rye and pumpernickel—long loaves of miniature slices, the foundation on which so many great hors d'oeuvres are built.

Champagne—provided it's allowed, it's worth the space it takes up in your fridge to keep on hand for that unexpected celebration.

Can of green chiles—a staple if you like "hot-n-spicy" Mexican food.

Lemon curd—a single dollop goes a long way. This sweet lemony sauce will perk up a store-bought pound cake.

Items Available on Campus.

Keep in mind ways to put your meal (board) plan to good use. Many colleges have a number of dining facilities where these items are available or where you can buy some of them à la carte. Some of these also will be available at a campus snack bar.

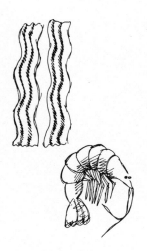

Strips of cooked bacon—great for salads, baked potatoes, egg salad, any sandwich or spread.

Shrimp, boiled and still in the shell— at Duke University, on Friday afternoons shrimp is available by the pound at our snack bar for Happy Hour. Super!

Crackers, individually packaged to go with soups—use for snacks and hors d'oeuvres

Orange juice—for breakfast and orange rolls

Coffee cream—sometimes you need only a little bit

Cartons of milk

Yogurt—for healthy fruit frappes, cold yogurt soups, tzatziki sauce

Fresh fruit—look for the regulars: apples, oranges, bananas, pears, grapes

Cream cheese

Salt and pepper packets

Ketchup and mustard packets—each
packet equals 1 tablespoon

Individual boxes of cereal for Apple
Crisp

breakfast & brunch

let's face it. College students sleep late! Most of us miss breakfast altogether. But rather than feeling self-conscious about your stomach rumbling so loud others can hear it (and it always does about halfway through your first morning class—right?), why not consider boiling up an egg in your hot pot or mixing a handful of granola in plain yogurt? Of course, keeping small boxes of cereal to have with milk is obvious, but see the box on page 34 for some instant breakfast yogurt concoctions that are easy to prepare, and which are a delicious answer to the empty stomach blues. Also, preparing the suggested bread and sweet roll

recipes in the evening, when you have more time, is a good way to ensure having something tasty to grab first thing in the morning.

Weekend breakfasts and brunches are an entirely different matter. I've found that late Saturday mornings in the fall (pre–football game) are one of the most popular times to entertain.

The key to a successful brunch is making sure you have all the ingredients on hand. Check this the day before—even if you have to stop at your favorite 24-hour mini mart on the way home from a date, it is far better than dragging yourself out of bed in the morning for that extra trip.

Incidentally, no brunch is complete without a good supply of bloody marys, screwdrivers, or mimosas, provided that you are of legal drinking age and dorm rules permit.

egg cups

fixing eggs in this manner leaves you free to finish getting ready in the morning or to put the final touches on other items for brunch. These can be easily prepared for individual servings, using aluminum foil cupcake tins or ovenproof glass custard cups. For a crowd, use a regular-size aluminum foil baking pan. Use 6 eggs and multiply the listed ingredients by 6. Bake for 20 to 30 minutes and test for doneness by jiggling the pan; it should be firm in the middle.

Baked eggs will puff up like a soufflé and taste like a mini omelet or a crustless quiche. Add any of the following for a gourmet touch: sliced mushrooms, diced tomatoes, shredded cheese, chopped onion or ham, or crumbled bacon. Serve baked eggs immediately, with buttered toast.

1 tablespoon butter
1 to 2 eggs
1 tablespoon milk or
*　　cream*
Dash of salt and
*　　black pepper*

1. Preheat your toaster oven to 375° F.

2. Place the butter in the cupcake tin, and place the tin in the toaster oven. As soon as the butter has melted, remove the tin from the oven and swirl the butter around to grease the bottom and sides. Set aside.

3. In a small bowl whisk together the remaining ingredients, and add any of the variations mentioned above. Pour the egg mixture into the greased tin.

4. Place the tin in the toaster oven and bake for 15 to 20 minutes. To test for doneness, jiggle the tin slightly: the egg should appear firm in the center.

Serves 1

homemade beer bread

I bet you never knew that making bread could be so easy! There's no yeast to worry about and no kneading or rising time is needed. This bread is delicious au naturel, or with butter. It is also great a few days later, reheated or as toast. Or even serve it as the base of a strawberry shortcake—just sprinkle a bit of sugar on the bread slices before topping with fresh berries and whipped cream. Since a regular-size loaf pan won't fit into your toaster oven, look for a set of aluminum foil mini loaf pans in the utensil department of your supermarket. They come in sets of three, are inexpensive, and can be reused.

3 cups self-rising flour
12-ounce can beer
3 tablespoons sugar

1. Preheat the toaster oven to 350° F.

2. Mix all the ingredients in a bowl until thoroughly combined. The batter will be fairly dry.

3. Grease well three mini loaf pans, and divide the dough equally among the three pans.

4. Bake for 40 to 45 minutes. Cool a few minutes before serving to make slicing easier.

Makes 16 to 18 slices

orange rolls

These are sticky but delicious. Serve them warm, with plenty of butter alongside. They are perfect for brunch or as a rich accompaniment to dinner. You will have to bake them in two shifts since all 12 won't fit in the toaster oven at once. Plan to throw away your aluminum foil baking pans, or line them with foil first, because they will be very gooey and difficult to clean.

---

*8 tablespoons
(1 stick) butter
1⅓ cups sugar
1 to 2 tablespoons
grated orange peel
1 to 2 tablespoons
orange juice
12 brown-and-serve
rolls (available in
the bread section
of the grocery
store)*

1. Preheat the toaster oven to 350° F.

2. Place the butter in a shallow ovenproof dish or aluminum foil pan and place it in the oven. Watch closely to make sure the butter does not burn. When the butter has melted, remove the pan and set it aside.

3. Mix together the sugar, orange peel, and orange juice. The mixture will be very crumbly.

4. Set up an assembly line: Start by dipping each roll into the melted butter, then roll it in the sugar mixture. "Pack" the sugar around and on top of the roll. Make a small break into the top of each roll and push some of the sugary goodies into the center, but be careful not to break the roll completely apart. Place the rolls, close together but not touching, on an aluminum foil pan.

5. Bake for 10 to 15 minutes, or until the sugar coating is bubbling and the rolls are golden brown.

Makes 12 rolls

donut drops

No yeast, no rolling—just fun, filling, delicious homemade donuts which I guarantee will be a big hit. Make the dough ahead of time and let your guests help you with the actual cooking.

*2 cups Bisquick
   baking mix
1 egg
1 teaspoon vanilla
   extract
¼ cup milk
¼ teaspoon ground
   cinnamon
¼ teaspoon baking
   powder (if you
   have it)
1 cup plus 2 table-
   spoons granulated
   sugar
½ cup powdered
   sugar
1 teaspoon ground
   cinnamon
16-ounce bottle
   vegetable oil
   (2 cups)*

1. Combine all the ingredients through the baking powder. Add the 2 tablespoons sugar and mix well. Make sure everything is well blended. Set aside.

2. Place the powdered sugar in one bag (a plastic bag or a small paper bag will be perfect) and the cinnamon and remaining granulated sugar in another bag.

3. Spread several layers of newspaper around your workspace to catch spills and drips. Pour the oil into your hot pot and turn the temperature setting to high. Allow the oil to heat for at least 5 minutes. To check if the oil is hot enough, carefully flick a small drop of water into the oil. If it sizzles, it is ready. Form Ping-Pong-size balls of dough in the palms of your hands. Carefully drop the dough balls into the oil a few at a time.

4. Turn the donuts over as they are cooking, and remove them from the oil when they are a uniform golden brown. Drain them on a plate covered with paper towels. Allow the donuts to cool for a few moments until you can handle them.

5. Drop each warm donut into one of the bags which contain the sugar toppings. Shake well to make sure the donuts are well covered. Remove from the bag and serve while still warm.

(To dispose of the oil, see page 87.)

Makes 25 small donuts

parmesan rolls

This is an interesting variation on the Orange Roll recipe, using Parmesan cheese instead of the sweet topping. For a particularly flavorful roll, buy Parmesan cheese by the piece and grate it yourself. This is definitely worth the effort. For a brunch variation, make 6 orange rolls and 6 Parmesan rolls. These also double as perfect dinner rolls.

*8 tablespoons
(1 stick) butter
1 dozen brown-and-
serve rolls
1 cup grated Parme-
san cheese*

1. Preheat the toaster oven to 350° F.

2. Melt the butter in a shallow pan in the oven as you did for the Orange Rolls.

3. Dip each roll in the melted butter, then in the grated cheese. Make a small break in the top of each roll and push a little cheese down into the center.

4. Arrange the rolls on an aluminum foil baking sheet, close together but not touching, and bake for 15 minutes, or until golden brown.

Makes 12 rolls

quick breakfasts

a favorite on campuses throughout the country, yogurt is healthful and nutritious, and *au naturel* it also has many uses in recipes that are especially suited to easy breakfasts.

- Add fresh fruit to plain or flavored yogurt.

- Pour a container over a half cantaloupe and sprinkle with granola and honey.

- Add yogurt to fruit drinks to make them more creamy and milkshake-like (see page 120, for one example).

- Use it to top your favorite morning cereal.

- Blend it with cottage cheese and spread it on warm toast with a dollop of your favorite jam or marmalade.

fluffy cheese soufflé

this elegant brunch entrée is a great way to use up a few odds and ends that may be in the fridge. Don't forget, though, to start a day ahead since this must sit overnight. It's definitely worth the advance planning.

2½ tablespoons butter, softened
3 slices white bread or leftover dinner rolls
4 ounces Cheddar cheese, grated
1 cup milk
2 eggs
½ teaspoon salt

1. Grease an aluminum foil baking pan with ½ tablespoon butter. Set aside.

2. Remove the crusts from the bread. Discard the crusts and generously butter each slice of bread on one side. Cut the buttered bread into small cubes.

3. Arrange the bread cubes in the baking pan in two layers, alternating with the grated cheese. Dot the top with any remaining butter. Set the pan aside.

4. In a small bowl, whisk together the milk, eggs, and salt. Pour this mixture over the bread and cheese. Cover the pan with plastic wrap and refrigerate overnight.

5. Bake in a preheated 275° F toaster oven for 45 minutes. Serve immediately.

Serves 4

french toast with orange syrup

$f$or a really gourmet touch at your next brunch, try this rich version of an old favorite. In smaller portions, it makes a nice dessert or a perfect accompaniment to tea. Serve the toast with traditional maple syrup, or for an exotic change, try the recipe for Orange Syrup which follows. Have all the toppings out and ready to serve ahead of time. The actual cooking is done at the last minute, so make sure your plates, silverware, napkins—and especially your guests—are ready.

---

1 egg
¼ cup milk
16-ounce bottle vegetable oil (2 cups)
4 slices pound cake (if frozen, make sure it is completely defrosted), or old bread, cut into pieces to fit the hot pot

Toppings:
½ cup powdered sugar
Ground cinnamon
Maple syrup
Orange syrup (recipe follows)

1. With a fork, beat the egg with the milk in a shallow bowl. Set aside.

2. Place the oil in your hot pot, plug it in, and turn the temperature to high. Spread newspapers on your desk top to catch any drips or spills.

3. To test if the oil is hot enough, place a drop of water on your finger and flick it into the pot. When it's hot, it will sizzle, and you're all set.

4. Dip the bread or pound cake into the egg mixture, covering both sides, and then place it in the oil. You can probably manage two at a time. Watch them closely—they don't take long. Turn the piece of cake or bread over when nicely browned, and then lift the pieces out of the oil with a fork or large spoon to a plate lined with paper towels. Allow to drain for a moment, then encourage people to start eating while you keep the assembly line going (or maybe each person could make his or her own, to get everyone in on the action). Top toasts with a sprinkle of powdered sugar and cinnamon and/or one of the syrups.

(To dispose of the oil, see page 87.)

orange syrup

make this ahead of time, and keep it in a jar in the refrigerator, if you have one. Then to warm it slightly, fill up a sink or large bowl with really hot water (since your hot pot is engaged with the oil for the French toast), and, making sure the jar is sealed, just submerge it in the water and let it sit until you are ready to serve it. (This is also delicious over ice cream.)

½ cup orange juice, or the fresh-squeezed juice of 1 orange
1 cup firmly packed brown sugar
2 tablespoons Grand Marnier or apricot brandy (optional)

1. Place the juice and sugar in the hot pot. Turn the temperature setting to medium and stir for about 5 to 10 minutes, until the sugar is dissolved.

2. Add the liqueur at the last minute and unplug the hot pot. Transfer the syrup to a clean jar, and allow the sauce to cool before covering it.

Serves 2 to 4

cheese biscuits

a unique variation on the southern biscuit, these are the perfect accompaniment to any brunch . . . or for any meal, really! Be sure to note all the serving ideas below.

1½ cups Bisquick or
*   other biscuit*
*   mix*
½ cup beer
½ cup grated
*   Cheddar or Swiss*
*   cheese*

1. Preheat the toaster oven to 375° F.

2. Combine all the ingredients in a small mixing bowl. It will be a dry mixture.

3. Shape the dough into little balls about the size of a Ping-Pong ball and place them on a greased aluminum foil baking sheet.

4. Bake for 15 minutes or until they are golden brown on the top.

For brunch: Serve hot in a napkin-lined bowl or basket, with lots of butter alongside.
For a picnic: Form slightly larger biscuits and use them instead of bread for sandwiches.
For hors d'oeuvres: Make tiny bite-size balls (reduce the baking time to 7 to 10 minutes) and serve on a plate with a bowl of tuna pâté or chicken salad (see pages 57, 75) in the middle; or use toothpicks to dip the biscuits in tzatziki sauce (see page 53).
As leftovers: Split, spread with butter, and broil in the toaster oven. This makes for a memorable breakfast.

Makes 6 to 8 biscuits

appetizers & anytime snacks

these recipes—from dips for crackers to a snazzy fondue—are easy to prepare at any hour of the day or night and are guaranteed to make your room a popular spot. They'll satisfy those between-meals cravings and keep you going when you're cramming for exams. And they're also great for a gathering in your room before the next dance or party.

QUICK, BRENDA, MORE HORS D'OEUVRES!

cheese fondue

One of my favorite recipes, this makes a substantial and delicious addition to an hors d'oeuvres party, or it can be a romantic dinner entrée. Don't worry if you don't have fondue forks. What would you use to roast marshmallows? Well, put those same ideas to work here: table forks (not plastic), straightened wire hangers, old barbecue skewers from home, etc.... But if fondues become a staple of your dorm-room cuisine, you'll probably want to buy real fondue forks—it's easy to find cheap ones.

1 pound Swiss cheese
¼ pound Gruyère cheese (see Note)
3 tablespoons all-purpose flour
¼ teaspoon garlic powder
Dash of black pepper
1½ cups dry white wine
1 loaf French bread, cut up into bite-size pieces with as much crust showing as possible (day-old bread is cheaper and works beautifully)

1. Grate both cheeses over a piece of wax paper, or if a grater is not available, sliver it fine with a knife. Empty the grated cheeses into a large plastic bag.

2. Add the flour, garlic powder, and pepper to the plastic bag and shake it well to combine the ingredients. If you have use of a refrigerator, you can do this ahead of time, then seal the bag and store it until right before your guests arrive.

3. Place the white wine in the hot pot and turn the temperature setting to medium. Just before it boils, sprinkle in the cheese mixture, a handful at a time, stirring constantly with a wooden spoon. When you have added all the cheese, reduce the heat by a few notches, so it is just above low.

4. Continue stirring until all the ingredients are well combined, of a homogeneous consistency, and "melty looking." This process will take several minutes, so don't lose your cool—or your confidence! Have

your guest(s) gather around, fondue forks in hand. When the fondue is ready, pass around the bread. Dip speared pieces of bread into the melted cheese mixture—and enjoy!

Note: Gruyère is a much stronger-tasting cheese, and probably more expensive, than regular Swiss. If you prefer not to use it, substitute an additional ¼ pound of Swiss.

Serves 4 to 6 as a meal, 12 as an hors d'oeuvre

artichoke dip

this is an all-star favorite from a friend of mine at the University of Cincinnati. I promise it will make artichoke lovers out of all your friends. It is guaranteed to be a big hit at your next party and it couldn't be any easier!

14-ounce can artichoke hearts, drained well and cut into small pieces
1 cup grated Parmesan cheese
1 cup mayonnaise
½ teaspoon garlic salt or garlic powder
Choice of crackers

1. Preheat the toaster oven to 425° F.

2. Combine all the ingredients, except the crackers, in the order given in a medium-size aluminum foil baking pan or an ovenproof serving dish.

3. Bake the artichoke dip for 25 minutes or until the top is golden brown and bubbly.

4. Remove the dip from the oven and allow it to cool for a few minutes before serving on crackers.

Makes 3 cups

baked brie with sautéed almonds

the following recipe will serve two to four people, depending upon how hungry they are. The proportions can be increased by buying a bigger wheel of cheese, etc. For an interesting variation, which can be a snack or a dessert, eliminate the nuts and butter; and after removing the brie from the oven, ice it with orange marmalade or apricot jam and serve with gingersnaps.

4-ounce round brie cheese (you'll find this in a little square box in the refrigerated-foods section)
½ loaf French bread
1 tablespoon butter
2 ounces sliced almonds (half of a small package)

1. Preheat the toaster oven to 325° F.

2. Remove all the wrappings from the cheese, but do not disturb the solid white rind. Wrap the cheese in aluminum foil, or place it in a small ovenproof bowl and then cover the bowl with foil. Pop it into the toaster oven for 15 minutes.

3. While the cheese is baking, slice the bread and arrange it in a basket or on a plate.

4. In the hot pot, melt the butter over low heat. Add the almonds and stir gently for a few minutes. Do not allow the almonds to get too brown.

5. Remove the cheese from the oven and transfer it to a plate, carefully removing the foil. Pour the sautéed nuts over the top of the cheese.

6. To serve, cut into the cheese with a sharp knife (it will be gooey and runny). Friends will love it spread on the bread slices.

Serves 2 to 4

creamy taco dip

a surprisingly simple interpretation of this Mexican-style dip. Serve with your favorite taco chip.

8-ounce package cream cheese, well softened
16-ounce container sour cream
1 envelope (1¼ ounces) taco seasoning mix
3 medium-size tomatoes, chopped into small pieces
1 small head lettuce, shredded or well chopped
Taco chips

1. Place the cream cheese, sour cream, and taco mix in a medium-size bowl, and mix well until it is smooth.

2. Either add the tomatoes and lettuce directly to the dip—mixing them in well—or place them in separate bowls and dip the chip first in the cream cheese mixture, then sprinkle with tomatoes and lettuce.

Makes 3 cups

PSSSST! TACO PARTY IN ROOM 308!

preparing crudités

The key to serving raw vegetables is to have them all at the peak of freshness. Vegetable strips, like those cut from celery and carrots, keep best in a shallow bowl of cold water in the refrigerator. Here are some basic steps for preparing and presenting raw vegetables, or as the French say, *crudités*. *Note:* A sharp knife and a vegetable peeler will come in handy here. First, wash all vegetables well, and allow the excess water to drain.

• **Cherry tomatoes** are ready to go after they have been washed and patted dry.

• **Carrots:** Peel the carrot and then trim both ends. The carrot may be either sliced into very thin rounds (if it is a large one) or cut lengthwise into narrow strips, approximately 3″ to 4″ long.

• **Snow peas:** Snap off the stem end and pull it back to remove the stringy fiber that runs along the seam side.

• **Green and red peppers:** Make a circular cut into the top of each pepper to remove the core. Shake out as many seeds as you can, and remove the rest of the seeds with your fingers. Cut the pepper in half and trim off any of the whitish fibrous material on the inside. Then cut the pepper into long thin slices.

• **Zucchini:** Trim both ends of the zucchini, and either cut it into rounds (about ¼″ thick) or lengthwise into long narrow strips. Leave the skin on.

- **Celery:** Remove each stalk from the heart of the celery. Remove any leaves and any stained areas. Holding one end, cut the stalk into three lengthwise strips and trim the strips to the length you wish, approximately 3″ to 4″.

- **Broccoli:** About 2½″ from the base of the flowerets, make one large horizontal cut to remove the bulk of the stalk. Then separate each clump into bite-size flowerets. Some of these will snap apart easily, others need to be cut.

- **Cucumber:** Trim off the ends and cut into rounds or long strips—peeled or unpeeled.

- **Cauliflower:** With a knife, make several cuts at the base of the head to remove the leaves. Still using the knife, cut each individual floweret away from the stalk, again remembering that they should be bite-size.

To serve *crudités*, arrange them artfully in little piles or clusters, ideally on a bed of leafy green lettuce.

baked pecan & cheese dip

So good it will take away your appetite for dinner. Serve it hot with crackers.

8-ounce package
 cream cheese,
 softened
5-ounce jar or
 package dried beef,
 chopped well
8-ounce container
 sour cream
1 very small onion,
 chopped
¼ cup chopped green
 pepper
2 tablespoons butter
½ cup chopped
 unsalted pecans or
 walnuts
Choice of crackers

1. Mix all the ingredients through the green pepper in an aluminum foil baking pan. Spread evenly in the pan. If you have use of a refrigerator, this could be done ahead of time and stored there, covered with plastic wrap.

2. Preheat the toaster oven to 375° F.

3. Turn the hot pot to a medium setting. Add the butter and when it has melted, add the chopped nuts. Sauté, stirring constantly, until the nuts turn a light golden color. Be careful not to let them burn. Remove the nuts and set them aside.

4. Place the aluminum pan with the cream cheese mixture in the toaster oven for 15 minutes. When the mixture is heated through, remove the pan from the oven and spoon the sautéed nuts on top. Return the pan to the oven for 5 to 10 minutes, or until the mixture is bubbly around the edges.

Makes 3 cups

quickie cheese puffs

This is the perfect pick-me-up for a study break snack. You can keep it on hand for when hungry friends stop by; the cheese mixture can be kept in the fridge for several days.

8-ounce package
   grated American
   cheese, or Velveeta
   cheese, grated
1 stalk celery, finely
   chopped
1 very small onion,
   finely chopped
½ cup mayonnaise
Salt and black pepper
1 loaf "party" rye or
   pumpernickel

1. Mix all the ingredients, except the bread, in a medium-size bowl. Set aside.

2. Tear a sheet of aluminum foil to fit your toaster oven, and arrange the slices of bread on it. Lightly toast both sides of the bread (one side at a time) in the toaster oven. Watch these closely, because it only takes a minute. (This is an important step, so that the bread will not become soggy.) Allow the bread to cool on the foil.

3. Place 1 heaping teaspoon of the cheese mixture on each slice of bread and spread evenly to the edges.

4. Broil the slices in the toaster oven for about 2 minutes, until the cheese is bubbly and just golden brown. Watch closely, since they burn easily. Serve immediately.

Serves 8 to 12

peppy swiss delights

this is perhaps the easiest and most consistently popular hors d'oeuvre recipe. The ingredients are so simple and inexpensive.

1 loaf "party" rye
Dijon mustard
(optional)
Two 4-ounce packages
sliced pepperoni
Two 8-ounce packages
sliced Swiss cheese

1. On sheets of aluminum foil, lightly toast both sides of the "party" rye (one side at a time) in the toaster oven. Remove from the oven, and allow to cool slightly

2. If you are using the mustard, spread a little on each slice of bread. Place two slices of pepperoni on each slice.

3. Trim the Swiss cheese into squares slightly smaller than the bread slices, and then place a slice of cheese on top of the pepperoni. You will have formed miniature open-face sandwiches which are ready for the toaster oven. If you have access to a refrigerator, you may want to do this much ahead of time and store them, covered, until you're ready to cook them.

4. To serve, preheat the broiler of your toaster oven and broil the little sandwiches on the same sheets of aluminum foil or on aluminum baking sheets. They are done when the cheese is brown and bubbly. You can probably fit 12 per sheet of foil in the toaster oven, so have several sheets of Peppy Swiss Delights ready to go.

Serves 8 to 12

spinach-stuffed mushrooms

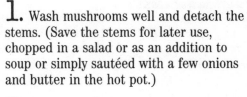

Serve these on a tray with drinks or other appetizers. Their pretty green color and delicate taste will impress your friends—and they need never know how simple the ingredients really were.

*24 medium to large
    fresh mushrooms*
*½ cup grated
    Cheddar cheese*
*12-ounce package
    Stouffers frozen
    Spinach Soufflé,
    completely
    defrosted*

1. Wash mushrooms well and detach the stems. (Save the stems for later use, chopped in a salad or as an addition to soup or simply sautéed with a few onions and butter in the hot pot.)

2. Dry the mushroom caps and arrange them on an aluminum baking sheet, bottom side up.

3. In a small bowl, mix the cheese with the defrosted spinach soufflé, using a wooden spoon. With a teaspoon, mound some of the spinach mixture onto the underside of each mushroom cap. If you have use of a refrigerator, this much can be done ahead of time and then stored, covered with plastic wrap.

4. Preheat the toaster oven to 400° F. Bake the stuffed mushrooms for 20 minutes, or until lightly browned.

Serves 8 to 10

mini onion sandwiches

f**or** this you want sweet onions, so choose Bermuda onions or ask your grocer for Vidalia onions, a particularly sweet variety. The result will be milder than you might think! (For crispy sandwiches, toast the bread lightly first.)

1 loaf "party" rye or very thin sliced bread
8 tablespoons (1 stick) butter, softened
1 medium to large sweet onion
½ cup mayonnaise
Seasoned salt or paprika

1. If you are using the very thin sliced bread, cut each slice into four pieces. On a sheet of aluminum foil or on an aluminum baking pan, arrange as many slices of bread as will fit. Spread each slice with butter.

2. With a very sharp knife, slice the onion as thin as you possibly can.

3. Arrange the onion slices on top of the buttered bread. You might have to cut the onions so that they will fit on the bread— don't worry if your onion slices are less than perfect. Place a very small dollop of mayonnaise on top of each onion sandwich (approximately ½ teaspoon). Sprinkle lightly with the seasoned salt or paprika. If you have access to a refrigerator, this much can be done ahead of time and stored, covered with plastic wrap, for a few hours.

4. To serve, preheat the broiler of your toaster oven and broil the onion sandwiches for a couple of minutes. Keep an eye on them so they do not burn, and remove the mini sandwiches from the oven when they are golden brown and the mayonnaise is bubbling.

Serves 6 to 10

pungent curry dip

the ingredients are a little unusual, perhaps, but the end result is well worth it—a pleasant surprise even for those who don't like curry. This can also be made well in advance of your party, and the leftovers can be saved too, since it keeps in the fridge for a week.

2 cups mayonnaise
3 tablespoons ketchup
3 tablespoons honey
3 teaspoons lemon juice
3 teaspoons curry powder
2 tablespoons very finely chopped onion

Combine all the ingredients in a medium-size bowl and stir well. Serve chilled with raw vegetables, such as carrots, celery, cauliflower, mushrooms, cucumbers . . . (See Preparing Crudités, page 44.)

Makes 2½ cups.

asparagus roll-ups

This is sure to please even those with the most discriminating palates, and the recipe also lends itself well to a host of variations. For example, you can add a slice of ham to the bread as you roll it up, or spread a little bottled horseradish sauce or spicy mustard on top of the cream cheese. Here's the basic recipe.

8 to 10 slices white bread
3-ounce package cream cheese, well softened
10½-ounce can asparagus tips or stalks, well drained and patted dry with paper towels
3 tablespoons butter

1. Trim the crusts from the bread slices. Then flatten each slice with your hands or by covering it with wax paper and placing a heavy book or your iron on top.

2. Spread the softened cream cheese on each slice of flattened bread, and place one asparagus stalk on each piece. Roll up the bread, jelly-roll style.

3. Cut the roll into halves or thirds—this will depend upon the original size of the bread—and place the pieces seam side down on an aluminum foil baking sheet. This much can be done ahead of time; cover with plastic wrap and refrigerate.

4. When you are ready to serve, preheat the toaster oven to 450° F. Place the butter in a small aluminum foil pan and put it in the oven just long enough for the butter to melt. Remove the pan and brush each roll with melted butter. Bake for a few minutes, watching carefully, until golden brown and heated through.

Serves 6 to 10

tzatziki

this is an exotic dip which I first tasted in Greece. For garlic lovers, it is the coup de grace! It is perfect as an accompaniment to a baked potato or as a dipping sauce for a fresh loaf of French bread or for some homemade Cheese Biscuits (see page 38). You can even serve it with fish.

1 small cucumber (about 6" long), peeled and thinly sliced
Salt
8-ounce container plain yogurt
2 cloves garlic, peeled and crushed, or ¾ teaspoon garlic powder

1. In a shallow bowl, arrange the cucumber slices in layers, salting each layer well. Allow this to sit for about an hour. The salt will release water from the cucumbers so that the sauce will not be too runny.

2. Meanwhile, mix the yogurt with the garlic in a medium-size bowl. Set aside.

3. Rinse the cucumber slices very well under cold water. Allow them to drain on paper towels, then pat dry.

4. Chop up the cucumber slices and place them in the bowl with the yogurt. Mix well, cover, and refrigerate for at least an hour. Serve very cold.

Serves 4

spinach dip in a rye bread bowl

Serve this dip chilled, with fresh raw vegetables, or for a creative touch, in a hollowed-out round loaf of rye or pumpernickel bread. (See steps 3 to 5 for details.)

*10-ounce package
frozen chopped
spinach,
completely
defrosted
1 cup mayonnaise
¾ package Knorr
Leek Soupmix
(about ½ cup)
1 teaspoon Italian
salad dressing mix
16-ounce carton
sour cream
1 loaf round rye
bread, unsliced
(optional)
Parsley sprigs for
garnish*

1. Once the spinach has defrosted, remove the wrappings and place the spinach in a clean old dish towel or in several layers of paper towels. Wrap it up and wring it as you would a washcloth so as to extract as much liquid as possible. Unwrap the spinach and place it in the container of your blender. Don't be alarmed if it looks as if there is only a little bit—the wringing compresses it into a little ball.

2. Add the other ingredients, through the sour cream, to the blender and blend until smooth. Serve the dip as is, or set aside and proceed with the following steps.

3. Cut a circle in the top of the loaf of bread, about 4 inches in diameter, and remove this piece. Using a sharp knife, spoon, or your hands, neatly scoop out the inside of the loaf, keeping the side (the crusts) intact. Set aside the insides.

4. Place the hollowed-out loaf on a plate and pour the spinach dip into the loaf as if it were a serving dish. Arrange parsley sprigs around the base of the loaf for a festive touch.

5. Cut the reserved bread into small bite-size pieces. Place them in a basket and use for dipping.

Note: When the dip is all gone, wrap the dip-saturated loaf and refrigerate it. For a special lunchtime treat the next day, cut the loaf into manageable pieces, and place them on an aluminum foil baking sheet. Broil these pieces in the toaster oven until the dip is golden brown and bubbly. This is a nice accompaniment to a mug of soup, and it uses up your leftovers!

Serves 6 to 8

egg salad

t o make egg salad, the cousin of the deviled egg, use the same ingredients I've listed on page 56. You'll find that egg salad is easier to transport to a picnic.

6 eggs
6 tablespoons mayon-
   naise, approxi-
   mately
Salt and black pepper
Optional extras: see
   page 56

1. Hard-boil the eggs, following the instructions in step 1, page 56. In a medium-size bowl, chop together the egg whites with the egg yolks, then add the mayonnaise, salt and pepper, and any of the other options.

2. Serve on your favorite bread for sandwiches, or use "party" rye to serve as an hors d'oeuvre or snack.

Serves 6

deviled eggs

d eviled eggs are great for snacks, picnics, hors d'oeuvres ... Add one or more of the optional extras to jazz them up accordingly. If this is a champagne occasion, for instance, add caviar!

6 eggs
6 tablespoons mayonnaise, approximately
Salt and black pepper
Paprika
Leaf lettuce, parsley sprigs, and lemon wedges for garnish

Optional:
Cooked bacon, crumbled
Finely chopped onion
Tabasco sauce
Dijon mustard
Sweet pickle relish
Lemon juice
Curry powder
Finely chopped green pepper
Finely chopped celery
Finely chopped parsley
Caviar

1. Place the eggs in your hot pot (it'll probably hold no more than six). Add at least 4 cups of water. Set the temperature to high and bring to a boil. Cover, reduce the heat to low, and continue cooking for an additional 10 minutes. Run cold water over the eggs to cool them down and halt the cooking process.

2. When they are cool enough to handle, shell the eggs and slice each in half lengthwise. Carefully scoop out the yolks and place them in a bowl. Mash the yolks well, then add the mayonnaise, a tablespoon at a time, until the consistency is creamy. Add salt and pepper to taste, and any of the optional extras you may want.

3. Arrange the halved egg whites on a tray. Spoon some of the yolk mixture into each egg white and sprinkle with paprika. Garnish the tray with lettuce, parsley, and lemon wedges. Serve well chilled.

Serves 4 to 6

tuna pâté

This adds a lot of elegance to an otherwise mundane item from your elementary-school days. Try it in a crock with crackers, as an open-face sandwich on pumpernickel bread for lunch, or in small individual portions with bread sticks as a first course.

Two 7-ounce cans
tuna, preferably
packed in water,
well drained
2 heaping table-
spoons plain
yogurt
Juice of 1 lemon
½ small onion,
chopped
Pinch cayenne or
black pepper

1. Place the tuna and the yogurt in the blender and process until smooth. Add the other ingredients and continue to blend until well combined.

2. Taste and correct the seasoning. Transfer to a bowl for serving. If you have a refrigerator, cover and chill it for an hour—the flavor will improve.

Serves 4 to 6

food for the great outdoors

College life can mean lots of picnics—before a ball game, in celebration of the coming of spring, or just to watch the leaves fall. So one indispensable item to have on hand is a picnic hamper of some kind. Whether it is an old beach bag, or a styrofoam cooler, or a real picnic basket doesn't matter—even a straw wastepaper basket can do double duty. Whatever, everyone loves a picnic as a nice change of pace.

There are all sorts of settings—an excursion to the beach or a nearby mountaintop, a romantic outing for two under a willow tree, or just somewhere quiet on campus. Picnic partners don't expect a lot of extras, but why not add a little panache next time?

Two standbys which automatically make picnics classy are real glasses and real cloth napkins—and even a colorful tablecloth. Brown grocery bags and white paper napkins work fine, of course, but if you want a special ambiance, go with the real thing. I'm certainly not suggesting lead crystal or heirloom linen—nothing even has to match. Maybe your family has a few odd wine goblets you can use. If not, it's easy to find inexpensive ones at pottery and glass outlet stores. The cloth napkins can be inexpensive, too.

If the picnic's going to include alcoholic drinks, I always recommend wine over beer. It gives a festive touch and will discreetly cover up any shortcuts you may have taken in your cooking. But always bring along something nonalcoholic, too, so there's a choice. And refer to the specialty items on page 23 when planning your "menu"— these will add a gourmet flavor. If you keep some exotic tidbits on hand, you will be prepared for that spur-of-the-moment occasion.

Many of the recipes in this book lend themselves perfectly to picnicking:

- Deviled Eggs or Egg Salad

- Taco Dip

- Curry Dip with fresh vegetables

- Oven-Baked Fried Chicken

- Chicken, Tuna Pâté, Ham Salad

- Gazpacho

- Marinated Vegetable Salad

- Lemon Squares

- Chocolate Cake

- Vanilla Pudding Cookies

- Chocolate/Peanut Butter No-bakes

- Sangria

- Mimosas

curried shrimp and egg pie

This chilled dip has a "crust" of cream cheese. Serve it with your favorite crackers.

8-ounce package
    cream cheese, well
    softened
3 tablespoons mayon-
    naise
½ teaspoon curry
    powder
6-ounce can shrimp,
    well drained
2 tablespoons lemon
    juice
2 eggs, hard-boiled,
    peeled, and
    chopped (see
    Deviled Eggs, page
    56)
¼ cup finely
    chopped scallions
1 tablespoon finely
    chopped celery
¼ cup finely
    chopped fresh
    parsley, plus a few
    sprigs for garnish
Freshly ground black
    pepper
Choice of crackers

1. Beat the cream cheese, mayonnaise, and curry powder with a wooden spoon until the ingredients are thoroughly combined and smooth.

2. Pack the cream cheese mixture into the bottom of a small shallow dish. Chill for 1 hour.

3. In the meantime, combine the shrimp, lemon juice, eggs, scallions, celery, and chopped parsley in a bowl. Toss well, and press this mixture into the chilled cream cheese. Garnish the dip with a few extra sprigs of parsley and a liberal sprinkling of freshly ground pepper.

4. Cover the bowl with plastic wrap and chill for at least 1 hour, or until ready to serve.

Serves 6 to 8

caviar pie

another super hors d'oeuvre (well seasoned in my grandmother's kitchen). Don't panic; it's not as expensive as you think! Because of all the yummy ingredients, you don't have to use the famed and pricey beluga caviar. Instead, use its distant and cheaper cousin, readily available in grocery stores. Your guests will still be impressed, and only the most discriminating palates can tell the difference.

3 eggs, hard-boiled, peeled, and well chopped (see Deviled Eggs, page 56)
1 small onion, finely chopped
8-ounce container sour cream
3½-ounce jar black caviar
Juice of 1 lemon
Crackers or melba toast

1. Layer the ingredients, except for the lemon juice and crackers, in the order given in a small shallow dish (a pie pan is perfect).

2. Squeeze the lemon juice over the caviar. Cover the dish with plastic wrap and refrigerate for at least 5 hours.

3. Serve the caviar pie with melba toast or your favorite crackers.

Serves 6 to 8

soup

for those who own a hot pot, soups could easily become the mainstay of a dorm-room kitchen. Adding some fresh ingredients to canned or dried soup will greatly enhance the flavor—particularly fresh tomatoes to tomato soup, finely chopped onions to leek soup, sliced mushrooms to mushroom soup, etc. If the recipe calls for water as the liquid, consider adding milk, or at least half milk and half water, to make it richer and more tasty. Any soup that has a cream or milk base can be spiked with a touch of sherry to give it a more gourmet flavor. A spoonful of sour cream, a sprinkle of either parsley, paprika or nutmeg, or a topping of chopped bacon or bread crumbs can be the final flourish.

Dry Soup Mixes. Knorr's (and other similar) dry soup mixes are wonderful bases to create hearty soups that will satisfy the hungry appetite.

• For leek soup, start with Leek Soupmix and instead of adding 4½ cups of water, substitute at least half that amount with milk, either whole or low fat. Then add up to ¼ cup of chopped onions (raw or sautéed) and up to 1 cup of diced potatoes (raw, cooked, or canned). If you use raw potatoes and onion, allow 1 hour cooking time on slow heat. If the onions and potatoes are cooked, just heat the soup and serve. (You could also add canned corn, drained.)

• For vichyssoise, follow the directions on the Leek Soupmix package, adding 1 can sliced potatoes, drained. When it has cooled completely, purée it in the blender. Serve very cold with a sprig of fresh parsley or some chives.

• For mushroom soup, add up to 1 cup of fresh mushrooms (washed, sliced, and sautéed in butter) and ¼ cup sautéed chopped onions or scallions to give the soup mix a heartier texture, or simply add 1 small can sliced mushrooms.

• To make a simple soup with only a few calories but lots of nutrition, add rice or barley, onion, leftover diced vegetables and meats, herbs, and a splash of wine or lemon juice to bouillon cubes or powder (either chicken or beef).

Canned Soups. One of my favorite canned soup variations begins with cream of tomato soup. First sauté half an onion, chopped fine, and 1 tomato, diced, in 1 tablespoon of butter in your hot pot. Then add 1 can cream of tomato soup. Fill the empty can with ¾ milk and ¼ sherry, and add this to the pot. Add a few parsley flakes and ¼ teaspoon ground nutmeg. Top with a spoonful of sour cream. Now you have a delicious tomato sherry bisque.

Another possibility is to combine different soups—like tomato and Cheddar cheese; cream of mushroom and cream of asparagus; cream of mushroom and chicken rice; beef vegetable with tomato. These are just a few suggestions; there are lots of possible combinations. You can also add tomato juice, V-8 juice, Worcestershire sauce, Tabasco, a pat of butter, herbs, curry powder, diced meats or vegetables, a ham bone, lemon peel, wine or sherry, cheese, mustard, garlic, bread crumbs, or crumbed bacon.

Don't be afraid to experiment and try different variations!

cold strawberry soup

Serve this unique chilled soup in bowls or teacups as a first course with a dollop of yogurt and a dash of nutmeg, or as a dessert accompanied by chocolates and delicate cookies. It also works well all by itself for a quick and refreshing pick-me-up.

Two 10-ounce containers frozen strawberries in syrup, defrosted
½ cup orange or apple juice
¼ teaspoon ground cinnamon
1 tablespoon lemon juice
16-ounce container plain yogurt

1. Place the strawberries with the syrup into the container of your blender. Blend until smooth.

2. Add the other ingredients in the order given and continue blending until well combined—smooth in texture and color.

3. Cover the soup and refrigerate for several hours. Give it a good stir before serving.

Serves 6

chilled tomato-yogurt soup

for a light lunch, serve this soup in bowls or mugs with a dollop of yogurt and a parsley sprig and perhaps some freshly ground pepper. Herbed Garlic Toast is a nice accompaniment.

*20-ounce can or bottle
    tomato juice
10-ounce container
    plain yogurt
2 cloves garlic, peeled
    and crushed, or ¾
    teaspoon garlic
    powder
Few drops Tabasco
    sauce
Salt and black pepper
Few sprigs fresh
    parsley, rinsed
    and chopped, for
    garnish*

1. In a large jar or bowl or blender, combine the tomato juice and the yogurt until smooth.

2. Add the garlic, Tabasco sauce, and salt and pepper and blend for a few more seconds.

3. Cover and refrigerate for several hours. Sprinkle with parsley and serve well chilled.

Serves 6

herbed garlic toast

Italian seasoning is a blend of herbs available in the spices section of the grocery store.

6 slices French or Italian bread
4 tablespoons (½ stick) butter
½ teaspoon garlic powder, or 2 cloves fresh garlic, peeled and crushed
1 teaspoon Italian seasoning
¼ cup grated Parmesan cheese

1. Arrange the bread slices on a sheet of aluminum foil.

2. In the hot pot, melt the butter on a low temperature setting. Add the garlic powder and Italian seasoning. Unplug the hot pot.

3. Spoon a little of the melted butter onto each slice of bread and carefully spread it to the edges.

4. Sprinkle some Parmesan cheese on top of each buttered slice and place the slices in the toaster oven.

5. Broil until golden brown. Serve immediately.

Serves 6

open-face sandwiches

nothing makes a better soup accompaniment than a sandwich, and serving sandwiches open-face somehow makes them seem more elegant. Starting with your favorite bread, or English muffins as a switch, you can prepare a variety of these sandwiches in your toaster oven. First toast the English muffin or bread on both sides till light golden brown. Now start to build your sandwich.

- Spread pizza sauce, ham, tuna, or chicken salad on toast, top with mozzarella cheese, and broil.

- Spread Dijon mustard, then horseradish sauce, 2 or 3 pieces of canned or leftover cooked asparagus, a slice of Muenster cheese. Broil.

- For open-face Reuben sandwiches, use corned beef, sauerkraut, Swiss cheese, and Thousand Island dressing. Broil.

- Dieters—put tomato slices on a sheet of foil, then add cucumber slices and seasoned salt and black pepper. Sprinkle Parmesan cheese on top and broil.

gazpacho

This salad-soup is a good way to use up vegetables left over from a party, and it will keep in the refrigerator for several days. You could also add green pepper, carrots, or cauliflower. Use your imagination, and adapt the quantities to your own preferences. If extra people arrive, simply add more V-8 or tomato juice.

¼ cup peeled and
   chopped cucumber
2 large ripe tomatoes,
   cored and cut into
   pieces
3 tablespoons
   chopped onion
¼ cup chopped
   celery
2 tablespoons
   chopped fresh
   parsley, or 1
   teaspoon dried
   parsley flakes
2 tablespoons oil (see
   Note)
2 tablespoons vinegar
   (see Note)
1 cup V-8 or tomato
   juice
½ teaspoon salt
Dash of black pepper
2 teaspoons lemon or
   lime juice
½ teaspoon paprika
   (optional)

Place all the ingredients into the blender. Put the lid on securely and blend, using a stop-start technique at 5-second intervals. You don't want to purée the soup, just to mix it together. Since this soup must be served well chilled, store it in the fridge right in the blender bowl, with the lid on.

Note: You can substitute 4 tablespoons bottled Italian salad dressing for the vinegar and oil.

Serves 4 to 6

main courses

for those of you who have a craving for something really substantial, something with a real home-cooked touch, an honest-to-goodness dinner as you remember the true meaning of the word, here's the answer.

Many of these recipes are long-standing favorites of mine and the quantities have been reduced and adapted to conform to the limitations of the dorm room; therefore they serve 2 to 4 persons in most cases. If you have access to regular kitchen facilities, especially an oven, feel free to double or triple the recipes to accommodate a larger crowd.

Serving a meal that has been prepared in your dorm room is quite an accomplishment, but main dishes don't have to be limited just to the suggestions in this chapter. Also keep in mind the many varieties of open-face sandwiches (see box, page 68). Toaster ovens were made for these half-dressed versions of old favorites—so much more attractive to serve, even if they are more challenging to eat.

starting with chicken

Chicken, and especially the white meat of the breast, is a fundamental ingredient of many delicious recipes. It lends itself perfectly to the limitations of dorm-room cuisine, because it can be cooked in so many different ways and added to so many things. A boneless chicken breast requires only 10 to 15 minutes' cooking time, and what's more, chicken is inexpensive, low in calories, and readily available in grocery stores.

For the greatest convenience, look for boneless chicken breasts. They usually come two or three to a package. To prepare the chicken for cooking, cut the breast halves apart, and trim off and discard fat or skin, if any. To make the chicken more tender and level out the thickness of the meat for more even cooking, cover the meat with plastic wrap and pound it flat with a heavy mug or beer stein. (You can skip the pounding if the chicken is being boiled for chicken salad or soup.)

Now the chicken is ready to cook. Keep in mind that for any of the following recipes, other chicken parts, such as legs, thighs, and breasts, with the bones intact, may be used. This of course will increase the cooking time substantially. It is always best to check chicken for doneness before you serve it. Here's how: With a small knife make a cut into the thickest part of the meat near a bone. Look at the juices—if they run clear, the chicken is done; if they are at all cloudy, pinkish or yellow, return it to the oven.

To Boil Chicken. The quickest method for cooking chicken is to boil it in your hot pot. The result is somewhat bland for just plain eating, but this is the ideal way to prepare chicken for chicken salad, sandwich spread, or as an addition to soups or vegetable dishes.

1. Bring 3 cups of water to a boil in the hot pot, and add 1 large chicken breast or 2 small ones. Keep the temperature high, but watch it carefully; you don't want it to boil over. Boil the chicken for 10 to 15 minutes.

2. Remove the chicken from the water and check for doneness. Unplug the hot pot and allow the chicken to cool thoroughly before deboning (if necessary) or proceeding with a recipe.

Add cut-up pieces of boiled chicken to Rice Casserole (see page 93), substituting chicken broth for beef broth; or add chicken to frozen broccoli au gratin or macaroni and cheese to make either into a meal.

Don't throw away the liquid or stock you cooked it in, since this could be the beginning of a wonderful soup: just add rice or barley; chopped carrot, celery and onion; chicken pieces;

and seasonings, such as dill, salt and pepper. Allow it all to stew in the hot pot on low for a few hours. Chicken stock may be stored in the refrigerator, covered, for up to one week, or if you have freezer space, it can be frozen for several months.

To Bake Chicken. Baking is another easy way of preparing chicken, and baked chicken is especially adaptable for entrées. Boneless chicken breasts will take only 30 minutes in a preheated 350° F oven; other chicken parts will take about 1 to 1½ hours at the same temperature. Be sure to check for doneness. Serve with noodles, rice, or a veggie steamed in your hot pot.

Note: If baking chicken breasts plain and without skin, be sure to rub the flesh with plenty of oil to prevent it from drying out while cooking.

To Broil Chicken. Broiling is another quick method of preparing chicken, best for boneless chicken breasts with the skin still attached. (In a toaster oven, because the food is so close to the heating coils, chicken parts with the bones still in them tend to burn on the outside before the center has had a

chance to cook.) It usually takes 15 minutes to broil a chicken breast. A brown, bubbly-looking surface on the outside is desirable, but do not allow it to get charred. Turn the chicken over and brown both sides. Broiled chicken, with its crisp skin, tastes great as is or with a squeeze of fresh lemon and a sprig of parsley. If you prefer, barbecue sauce, straight from the bottle, is great to use for basting as you cook. Be sure to have plenty of extra sauce on hand to serve with the chicken.

chicken salad

Serve this on a bed of lettuce or as a sandwich on your favorite bread. It is not crucial to include all of the ingredients—chicken and mayonnaise are the mainstays.

2 to 3 chicken breast halves, boiled (see page 72) and cut into small chunks, or 2 cups chopped leftover chicken
½ cup chopped celery (1 stalk)
¼ cup raisins, or ½ cup seedless green grapes, cut lengthwise
½ cup drained crushed pineapple
2 tablespoons lemon juice
¼ cup roughly chopped unsalted walnuts
3 heaping tablespoons mayonnaise, or enough to bind ingredients together

Mix all the ingredients in a medium-size bowl until well combined. Serve chilled.

Serves 2 to 3

Note: For a delicious sandwich, salad entrée, or hors d'oeuvre on crackers or melba toast, follow the recipe for Chicken Salad, substituting 12 ounces chopped ham for the chicken.

chicken pâté

$t$his delicious pâté is a variation for those who are not liver-lovers. So easy and so versatile—serve it chilled in a crock with crispy crackers for those times when you want hors d'oeuvres to double as dinner; or spread it on fresh bread with a little lettuce and tomato for a gourmet sandwich.

*2 chicken breast
    halves, boiled (see
    page 72) and cut
    into ½" pieces*
*¼ tart apple, peeled,
    cored, and cut into
    chunks*
*1 scallion, chopped
    fine, or 1 table-
    spoon finely
    chopped onion*
*8 tablespoons
    (1 stick) butter,
    softened and cut
    into 6 pieces*
*1 teaspoon lemon
    juice*
*¼ teaspoon curry
    powder (or if
    you're not wild
    about curry,
    substitute chili
    powder or cayenne
    pepper)*
*Fresh parsley sprigs,
    for garnish
    (optional)*

1. Place the chicken pieces in the blender. Add the apple and the scallion and blend, using stop-start intervals. Scrape the sides of the container with a rubber spatula.

2. Add the remaining ingredients except the parsley, and continue blending until the mixture is smooth.

3. Taste the pâté. You may want to add some salt and pepper. Transfer the pâté to a crock or small bowl, and smooth out the top with a knife so that it is level with the rim of the bowl. Cover with plastic wrap and chill. Garnish with fresh parsley sprigs before serving.

Serves 2 to 3

marinated baked chicken

4 boneless chicken breast halves, or 4 to 6 other pieces
1 bottle Italian salad dressing

1. At least 8 hours before you plan to serve the chicken, but preferably the day before, rinse the pieces and pat them dry. Place the uncooked chicken parts in a bowl. Pour the salad dressing over the chicken, cover the bowl with plastic wrap, and place it in the refrigerator and allow to marinate.

2. To cook it, place the chicken in an aluminum foil baking pan, and bake according to the instructions on page 73. This is delicious cold for a picnic, or take it along and cook it over a picnic grill.

Serves 2 to 3

ambiance, atmosphere, aesthetics

have a look around your room. Do you think there's just no way you could entertain anyone there. Maybe you don't have the right serving utensil or there's a cheap overhead neon light (or, more likely, a bare bulb). For heaven's sake, don't worry about it! What follows are a few ideas which will certainly add to the atmosphere and ambiance of your next get-together or party.

• **Make up a holiday in honor of the occasion.** I'm Learning to Cook Day, Number of Days Until School's Out, A Halfway Birthday Party for a friend whose birthday falls in the summertime, Midterm Recovery Day . . . whatever it takes to fit your fete! Any of these would be a great way to launch your career as a campus cook.

• **Set the mood with the invitation.** This will create intrigue as to what you've been up to in that "kitchen" of yours! Follow through with the decorations, matching the food to the theme.

YOU'RE INVITED TO A
MYSTERY DINNER
in my room (308)6th
Saturday Night

- **Candles help tremendously.** Remember, everyone looks good in candlelight—and your guests will love the dramatic ambiance they add. Use candles all over—carefully.

- **Create a party centering around one food item,** like an Apple Party in the fall. You could serve hot cider with cinnamon sticks, apple crisp, dip apples in chocolate fondue, etc. Other possible theme parties might be Mexican, Irish, Tropical, Oriental, and so on. If you can get a few friends interested in dorm cooking, you could have a progressive dinner party, where you go to a different room for each course. The possibilities are endless, and the more imaginative, the better!

- **Real flowers of any kind work wonders.** Daisies are inexpensive and you need only a few, or maybe you know of a spot along the roadside where you can pick some wildflowers. Put the flowers in any sort of a container—even plastic cups are fine. Your friends will be looking at the flowers, not at the vase.

creamy baked chicken

4 boneless chicken
  breast halves, or 4
  to 6 other pieces
1 can condensed
  mushroom soup
½ cup milk
6 fresh mushrooms,
  washed and sliced
  thin
2 tablespoons
  chopped onion
2 tablespoons
  chopped celery
½ teaspoon dried
  parsley flakes
Salt and black pepper

1. Rinse the chicken pieces and pat them dry. Arrange the chicken in an aluminum foil baking pan so that the pieces are touching. Set aside.

2. Combine the mushroom soup with the milk in a small bowl. Add the vegetables and stir gently. Pour the mixture over the chicken.

3. Sprinkle the parsley flakes over the top, and add salt and pepper to taste. Bake according to the instructions on page 73.

Serves 2 to 3

chicken nouvelle american

this version has a very delicate flavor. It goes very well with rice that has been cooked in chicken broth.

4 boneless chicken breast halves
4 tablespoons (½ stick) butter
3 tablespoons lemon juice or white wine
3 tablespoons finely chopped scallions
6 fresh mushrooms, sliced thin
Salt and black pepper
A few slivered almonds
Parsley sprigs, for garnish
Lemon wedges or slices, for garnish

1. Arrange the chicken in an aluminum foil baking pan so that the pieces are touching. Set aside.

2. Melt the butter with the lemon juice or wine in the hot pot on medium heat. Add the scallions and mushrooms, place the lid on the hot pot, and simmer the mixture for a few minutes, until the vegetables are tender. Then pour the sauce over the chicken, and add salt and pepper to taste.

3. Bake the chicken according to the instructions on page 73. In the last 5 minutes of baking time, sprinkle the almonds over the top and allow them to brown, but not burn. Garnish with parsley sprigs and lemon wedges.

Serves 2 to 3

oven-baked fried chicken

this makes a hearty main dish and the leftovers are great for lunch the next day. You might want to prepare it ahead of time and serve it cold for a traditional picnic. This recipe tastes just as though you had fried it, but without the mess. *Note:* The chicken used in this recipe should still be on the bone, with its skin attached.

4 chicken breast halves, or 4 to 6 other pieces
8 tablespoons (1 stick) butter
2 cups crumbled herb-seasoned stuffing (such as Pepperidge Farm) or bread crumbs, or 3 individual-serving-size boxes corn flakes, crushed
Dried herbs or spices—such as parsley, dill, basil, oregano, garlic powder
Seasoned salt and seasoned pepper

1. Rinse the chicken pieces well and pat dry with paper towels. Trim off and discard any excess fat or skin. Set the chicken aside.

2. Preheat the toaster oven to 375° F.

3. Melt the butter in the hot pot on a medium setting. Watch it closely to make sure it does not burn. When the butter has completely melted, unplug the hot pot and pour the butter into a small bowl suitable for dipping.

4. Spread several layers of newspaper on your tabletop or desk top to catch spills. Cover them with a sheet of wax paper. Place the stuffing, bread crumbs, or corn flakes on the wax paper. Add your choice of herbs to the bread crumbs.

5. Set up an assembly line: first dip the chicken in the melted butter, then roll it in the crumbs, then arrange it in an aluminum foil baking pan. Fit the chicken compactly, so that the pieces are touching or even overlapping.

6. Sprinkle the chicken liberally with the seasoned salt and pepper. Bake in the toaster oven for 1½ hours. Check for doneness by making a cut into the meat near the bone. The juices should be clear. If they are pinkish or yellow, return to the oven and continue baking for a few more minutes, then test again.

Serves 3

lemon-broiled chicken

*4 boneless chicken
    breast halves, or 4
    to 6 other pieces*
*4 tablespoons
    (½ stick) butter*
*3 tablespoons lemon
    juice, or the juice
    of 1 fresh lemon*
*1 tablespoon Worces-
    tershire sauce*
*1 tablespoon honey
    (optional)*
*1 tablespoon soy
    sauce (optional)*

1. Rinse the chicken pieces and pat them dry. Place the chicken in an aluminum foil baking pan so that the pieces are touching. Set it aside.

2. Combine all the remaining ingredients in your hot pot on medium-low heat. Once the butter has completely melted, unplug the hot pot and pour the liquid over the chicken.

3. Broil according to the instructions on page 73, basting several times with the sauce. Spoon a little of the sauce over each piece of chicken as you serve it.

Serves 2 to 3

fish filets cooked in foil

this is a fantastically easy recipe which is great for a dorm-room dinner. Serve it with rice and a fresh veggie steamed in the hot pot. If you are buying frozen fish, be sure to buy the unbreaded variety, allowing ⅓ to ½ pound per person.

4 thick fish filets, such as cod or haddock
4 tablespoons (½ stick) butter, softened
Any or all of the following herbs: parsley, basil, garlic salt, seasoned pepper or lemon pepper
1 medium onion, chopped fine
¼ cup fresh lemon juice (approximately 1 to 2 lemons), or ½ cup dry white wine
1 lemon, cut into wedges, for serving

1. Remove all the store wrappings from the fish and allow it to defrost completely.

2. Preheat the toaster oven to 400° F.

3. Rinse the fish with cold water to remove any "fishy" taste. Pat it dry with paper towels, and place each filet on a separate piece of heavy-duty aluminum foil. You may need to cut the filets into smaller pieces so that each sheet of foil contains one serving of fish.

4. Spread the fish with the softened butter, and sprinkle some of the herbs on top, according to taste. Also add a tablespoon of the chopped onion and distribute the lemon juice or wine equally among the four filets. Wrap the fish up in the foil as you would a package, making sure that the liquid does not leak out.

5. Place the foil packages in the toaster oven and bake for 20 minutes. Eat the fish right out of the foil.

Serves 4

grandma's meat loaf

The all-time outstanding meat loaf recipe straight from my grandmother's recipe file. Serve it as a main course for someone with a hearty appetite, or make it a day ahead of time and have meat loaf sandwiches on a picnic. Since a regular-size loaf pan won't fit into the toaster oven, you may be wondering how you're going to pull this feat off. Look in the utensils department of the grocery store for mini-size loaf pans. They usually come three to a set. You can stick with the disposable aluminum foil type, or perhaps you will want to invest in more sturdy, reusable, "real" pans. In any case, all three mini pans will fit into the toaster oven at one time.

Meat Mixture:
⅔ cup milk
1½ pounds lean
   ground beef
1 small onion,
   chopped fine
1 egg
½ cup cracker
   crumbs or crushed
   corn flakes
2 tablespoons finely
   chopped green
   pepper
2 tablespoons ketchup
2 teaspoons salt
½ teaspoon black
   pepper
1 teaspoon sugar

1. Preheat the toaster oven to 350° F.

2. Scald the milk: Place it in your hot pot and turn the temperature setting to medium-high. Watch it closely: when it begins to steam, the milk is scalded. Do not allow it to boil. Unplug the hot pot and allow the milk to cool.

3. Place the remaining meat mixture ingredients in a large mixing bowl.

4. Add the scalded milk to the meat mixture. With a large spoon or with your hands, mix everything together until it is well combined.

5. Divide the meat mixture evenly among the three loaf pans, forming little loaves with your hands. Place all three pans in the toaster oven.

(recipe continued on next page)

Sauce:
3 heaping table-
spoons brown
sugar
¼ cup ketchup
1 teaspoon dry
mustard, or 1
tablespoon
prepared mustard
¼ teaspoon ground
nutmeg (optional)

6. Combine all the sauce ingredients in a small bowl, and stir well until the sugar is dissolved. After the loaves have been cooking for at least 30 minutes, spoon some of the sauce over the top of each loaf. Continue to baste from time to time.

7. Bake the meat loaves for 1½ hours total.

Serves 4 to 6

beef fondue

this elegant classic can become a standard favorite in your dorm room, because it is so easy, so delicious, and so sociable. Don't worry about fancy fondue pots or forks—use your hot pot, and whatever you would use for roasting marshmallows, like a coat hanger, will work as a fork. Wrap a napkin around the handle if the fork gets too hot. Attach little name tags so that your friends will know whose hanger is whose.

Set the hot pot on the table or floor on top of a few newspapers to catch any drips or splatters. Seat your guests in a circle around the pot with the meat, sauces, and other food in the center also. They can balance their plates on their laps. Serve a tossed salad of fresh greens and a loaf of fresh French bread with the fondue to make a meal.

6 to 8 ounces fondue
beef per person
16-ounce bottle
vegetable oil
(2 cups)
Dipping sauces
(see box, page 88)

1. Pour the entire bottle of oil into your hot pot. Turn the temperature setting to high. Wait about 5 to 10 minutes, allowing the oil to become quite hot.

2. Test the temperature of the oil by carefully flicking a small drop of water into it. If it sizzles, it's ready to go, and you can reduce the heat to medium high. Otherwise, wait a few more minutes.

3. Each guest places several pieces of the raw meat on his or her plate, skewers one piece at a time onto the fork, and submerges it in the oil to cook. It takes only a few seconds, so don't get distracted.

4. Dip each cooked piece into one of the sauces and eat up!

Cleanup. Do *not* pour the oil into the toilet or down the sink or out the window. It won't take long to track the clog in the plumbing to your room. I suggest that you use the following technique: Allow the oil to cool completely. Make a cone using several thicknesses of newspapers, and hold this cone over the garbage can—ideally one with a heavy-duty plastic liner, like one in your hall. Pour the oil slowly into the cone and it will be completely absorbed by the newspapers. Before washing the pot, wipe it out several times with paper towels to absorb as much of the oil as you can. Then proceed to wash it normally.

keys to a great fondue

the key to a really successful fondue is to buy the best meat you can afford. Obviously filet is the best, but sirloin or top round will work just fine too. (Stewing meat, like chuck, is too tough to cook in this manner.) Allow ½ pound of meat per person. Ask the butcher or the person at the meat counter in the supermarket to cut the meat into bite-size pieces, to save yourself one more step back at the dorm room.

The second key is to have a wide variety of sauces from which your guests may choose. A selection of your favorite steak sauces will make a super start; others you might want to consider are:

- Sweet or spicy mustard

- Sauce Louis (combination of ½ cup mayonnaise, ½ cup ketchup or chili sauce, ½ teaspoon lemon juice, and ¼ teaspoon horseradish)

- Horseradish sauce (1 cup Cool Whip or whipped cream or even sour cream, blended with 1 teaspoon horseradish or to taste)

- Garlic butter (butter melted and flavored with garlic powder to taste; for every 8 tablespoons—1 stick—butter, add approximately ½ teaspoon garlic powder)

Put each sauce in an individual bowl for dipping.

vegetables & salads

mushy vegetables, limp salads, and pasty mashed potatoes are common problems at most college and university cafeterias. As a change from these bland, poor-quality vegetable dishes, the recipes listed in this chapter are unusual, healthful, and uncomplicated, and could even be the basis of an entire meal.

Don't forget that your hot pot doubles nicely as a steamer for fresh vegetables: Place about ½ cup of water in the bottom on a medium-high setting. Since it takes only a few minutes (a maximum of 10), steaming broccoli, asparagus, green beans or whatever can be

done at the last minute. Serve with a little butter, some fresh-squeezed lemon juice, and a few slivered almonds as a special treat for a cafeteria-weary friend.

Cheese also is a good accompaniment for fresh vegetables. Top yours with freshly grated Swiss, Cheddar, or Parmesan. Or a good standby is a small jar of Cheez Whiz. When heated, it becomes a delicious cheese sauce for any freshly steamed vegetable. Simply spoon a little onto the vegetable as you serve it and the heat will do the rest.

onion rings

Onion rings no longer have to be a special treat available only at restaurants. You can make this light, crunchy batter very easily in your hot pot. Buy the sweetest variety of onions you can find (ask your grocer for his recommendation). Prepare Pungent Curry Dip (see page 51) or use bottled ranch salad dressing for dipping. Dijon-type mustard or Nance's mustard sauce also works well. Strips of zucchini, mushrooms, broccoli flowerets, even shelled shrimp can be prepared this way as well as onions.

2 to 3 medium onions
1 cup Bisquick
   baking mix
¾ cup beer
1 egg
2 shakes Worcester-
   shire sauce
Dash of salt and
   pepper
1½ to 2 cups vegeta-
   ble oil

1. Peel the onions and slice them as thin as possible. Separate the rings and make a pile on a sheet of wax paper.

2. Whisk together in a small bowl the Bisquick, beer, egg, Worcestershire sauce, and salt and pepper until well combined. The mixture will be thick. If it gets too thick, you can always add an extra table-spoon of beer or water.

3. Cover your desk or work surface with several layers of newspapers to catch any drips of batter or oil. Place your hot pot in

the center of the papers. Pour the oil into the hot pot, and turn the temperature setting to high. Line a plate with a few layers of paper towels. This will be the draining plate for the cooked onion rings.

4. You'll want to set up an assembly line for this—onions, batter, hot pot. As you dip the onions into the batter, make sure you coat them completely. Then drop the onion rings into the oil. Test a small one first, to make sure the oil is hot enough. It should sizzle a lot as soon as you put the batter-dipped onion into the oil. With a wooden fork or spoon, keep turning the onions over, until they are a uniform golden brown. Remove the onion rings from the oil and let them drain on the paper towels. Since the cooking is an ongoing process, serve them as soon as they're ready, while they're still warm and crispy. Use the sauces to dip. (See page 87 for disposing of the oil.)

Serves 6

spinach balls

These can be made ahead and then popped into the oven just before serving. They make a great vegetable side dish for any meal, or a hearty appetizer. Serve with Tzatziki sauce (page 53) and/or Dijon mustard for dipping.

10-ounce package frozen chopped spinach, completely defrosted

1 cup crumbled herb stuffing (such as Pepperidge Farm), crushed

3 eggs, beaten with a whisk or fork

1 clove garlic, peeled and crushed, or ½ teaspoon garlic powder

Dash of grated nutmeg (optional)

½ teaspoon salt

6 tablespoons (¾ stick) butter, softened

½ cup grated Parmesan cheese

1. Remove the wrapping from the spinach. Squeeze out as much excess water as you can with your hands, then place the spinach in a dishcloth or towel. Wring it as you would a washcloth to get rid of all the water. Don't worry if the spinach has shrunk into a tiny ball.

2. Place the spinach in a medium-size bowl, and add the remaining ingredients except for the Parmesan cheese. Stir well with a large spoon or with your hands, making sure that all the ingredients are well combined.

3. Form the mixture into 1" balls and place them on a greased aluminum baking sheet that will fit into your toaster oven. Cover with plastic wrap and refrigerate until ready to serve.

4. Just before baking, preheat the toaster oven to 400° F. Roll each spinach ball lightly in the Parmesan cheese and replace it on the baking sheet. Bake for 10 to 15 minutes; test one to make sure it is heated through.

Serves 4 to 6

rice casserole

terrific for chilly winter nights and so easy. Team this up with a meat dish and you'll have a filling meal.

---

5 tablespoons butter
1 cup rice
1 small onion, diced
Two 10¾-ounce cans
*   condensed beef*
*   broth, undiluted,*
*   or 4 beef bouillon*
*   cubes dissolved in*
*   2 cups boiling*
*   water*

1. Preheat the oven to 325° F.

2. Melt the butter in an aluminum foil pan (with sides at least 2″ high) in the toaster oven, watching closely so the butter doesn't burn.

3. Remove the pan from the oven and add the other ingredients in the order given.

4. Bake for 1 hour. Fluff up the rice with a fork before serving.

Serves 4

snow pea-cucumber salad

this refreshingly different "lettuceless" salad is appealing both to the eye and to the palate. This recipe should start you thinking about other salad combinations you can create to break the iceberg lettuce routine. Serve it on individual plates or in a large salad bowl.

2 firm cucumbers, about 6" long
1/4 pound fresh snow peas
1/4 pound Jarlsberg cheese
Several sprigs fresh parsley or watercress
1 tablespoon wine vinegar or white vinegar
1 teaspoon Dijon mustard
3 tablespoons oil
Pinch of salt
Pepper, freshly ground if possible
A sprinkling of your favorite herbs

1. With a vegetable parer, peel the cucumbers and discard the skin. Continue using the parer to make paper-thin lengthwise slices of cucumber, stopping when you get to the seedy center. Discard the column of seeds which remains. Arrange the slices in a pile in the center of your bowl, or divide them evenly among individual plates.

2. Wash the snow peas well, and allow them to drain on paper towels. Snap off the stem end of each pea pod and pull along the seam to remove the tough, stringy fiber. Arrange the peas in a ring around the pile of cucumbers.

3. Remove the rind from the cheese and slice the cheese into long, thin pieces, a bit larger than matchsticks. Arrange the cheese in a narrow ring between the peas and the cucumber.

4. Break the parsley into miniature sprigs and toss them on top of the salad. Cover the salad and refrigerate, if possible, until ready to use.

5. To prepare the dressing, whisk together all the remaining ingredients in a small bowl. Set aside. Just before serving, toss the salad lightly with the dressing.

Serves 4 to 6

marinated vegetable salad

Serve as a vegetable side dish, or bring it along on a picnic. Be sure to start it a day ahead of time.

1 bunch fresh broccoli
6-ounce jar
* marinated*
* artichoke hearts,*
* undrained*
¼ pound fresh
* mushrooms,*
* washed and sliced,*
* or one 6-ounce jar*
* or can, drained*
10-ounce box frozen
* brussels sprouts,*
* defrosted and*
* drained (optional)*
½ cup bottled Italian
* dressing*

1. Fill your hot pot with water and bring it to a full boil.

2. Trim away the broccoli stems and cut the flowerets into bite-size pieces (see page 44). Toss them into the boiling water, just to blanch them. This takes only about 2 minutes, so watch carefully. The broccoli will turn from a dull green to a bright spring-green color. As soon as the broccoli is bright green, drain the boiling water away. Place the flowerets on a plate lined with paper towels to cool and drain.

3. Cut the artichoke hearts into pieces and place them, along with their liquid, into a large bowl together with the mushrooms, brussels sprouts, and the dressing. Add the broccoli and mix well. Cover and refrigerate, at least overnight.

Serves 4 to 6

salade niçoise

This famous salad's name indicates its gourmet origin—Nice, France, an area known for its delicious food.

Salad:

1 head leafy lettuce such as romaine, washed and patted dry

9-ounce can white tuna fish packed in water, drained

3 small tomatoes, cored and quartered

3 hard-boiled eggs, peeled and quartered (see page 56)

1 sweet red pepper, cut into fine julienne strips

10-ounce package frozen French-cut green beans, defrosted and drained

10 black olives, pitted

¼ pound sliced ham cut into fine julienne strips

4 new potatoes, boiled in the hot pot until tender, cooled, and quartered

1 can anchovy filets, drained

1. Arrange all the salad ingredients on a large plate in the order given: Line the plate with the lettuce; place the tuna in the center, and arrange the other ingredients in little piles around the tuna. The anchovies go on last: crisscross two filets on top of the tuna.

2. Whisk the dressing ingredients together in the order given, and drizzle it over the salad.

Serves 2 to 4

Dressing:
*3 tablespoons red
    wine vinegar*
*1 clove garlic, peeled
    and crushed, or ½
    teaspoon garlic
    powder*
½ teaspoon salt
*Freshly ground black
    pepper*
1 cup light olive oil

vegetables with lemon curd

this odd combination makes for a delicious vegetable salad sandwich. Lemon curd is a sweet creamy sauce that comes in a 10-ounce jar; you'll find it in the gourmet foods section of the supermarket or at most specialty foods shops. Usually used for desserts, it lends a tangy contrast to this recipe.

*1 slice whole-wheat
    bread*
*1 to 2 ounces cream
    cheese, softened to
    spread*
*6 slices unpeeled
    cucumber*
*½ tart apple, sliced
    paper thin*
*2 fresh mushrooms,
    sliced*
*Few fresh alfalfa
    bean sprouts*
*Generous dollop
    lemon curd*

Toast the bread in the toaster oven. Spread the cream cheese on the bread and arrange the other ingredients on top of the cream cheese in the order given.

Serves 1

baked potatoes plus

"**t**ater bars" and restaurants that feature stuffed baked potatoes seem to be springing up all over the place. Why go out to eat and pay extra for potatoes when you can prepare them easily and inexpensively in your dorm room? Buy medium-size baking potatoes—preferably Idaho, but any kind will do—and wash and dry them thoroughly. Bake them in your toaster oven at 400° F for 1 to 1½ hours. To test for doneness, see if you can easily insert a table fork into the potato. Remove the potatoes from the oven and split them in half. Pinch each half enough to loosen the flesh from the skin, and to make a small pocket for stuffing. Here is where the creativity and all the variations begin. (This is also a good way to use up leftover ingredients from previous culinary "indulgements" and any other tidbits in your fridge.)

Butter, of course, is the perfect partner for potatoes, but the possibilities and combinations are endless. Serve stuffed baked potatoes as a side dish or as a meal, depending upon the filling and how high you pile it on.

THE WEEK'S MENU IN ROOM 308

MON– CREAMED POTATOES
TUES– BAKED POTATO W/CHEESE
WED– POTATO SALAD
THURS– POTATO SOUP
FRI– BAKED POTATO W/SOUR CREAM
SAT– POTATO SURPRISE
SUN– POTATOES DEJA VU

Here are some stuffing ideas:

- Avocado chunks sprinkled with seasoned salt and seasoned pepper

- Grated cheese, almost any kind: Swiss, Cheddar, Colby, Parmesan, or processed cheeses like Cheez Whiz or other party cheese spreads, which will melt and form a sauce

- Bacon crumbles; leftover sandwich makings like bologna, ham, salami, pepperoni; even tuna fish

- Diced onion, green pepper, celery, cherry tomatoes, mushrooms, or any other raw vegetable, sautéed first in a little butter (and a little white wine for added gourmet flavor)

- Sour cream, yogurt, salad dressing, mayonnaise, or tomato sauce of any kind

- Leftover egg salad, ham salad, tuna salad, or any party dips from ranch salad dressing to Tzatziki (see page 53)

- Steamed fresh vegetables such as broccoli, cauliflower, or peas

- Condensed soups like cream of tomato or cream of mushroom (do not add water or milk—just heat in the hot pot and serve)

- Caviar, shrimp, or crab for the ultimate touch of elegance

potato-broccoli salad

If you're tired of the generic potato salad, made with gobs of mayonnaise, try this innovative combination for a great change from the routine.

10-ounce package frozen broccoli flowerets
1½ pounds new red potatoes, washed and cut into 1" cubes
4 tablespoons lemon juice
1 heaping teaspoon Dijon mustard
½ teaspoon salt
½ cup light olive oil
3 eggs, hard-boiled, peeled, and chopped (see page 56)
¼ cup chopped fresh parsley

1. Remove the broccoli from the freezer and discard the wrappings. Allow the broccoli to defrost completely, and drain.

2. In your hot pot, bring 4 cups water to a boil. Add as many potatoes as will fit without the water boiling over, and allow the potatoes to cook for 8 to 10 minutes until a fork can be easily inserted. Be careful not to allow the potatoes to become mushy. When done, fish out the potatoes from the boiling water and place them in a large bowl to cool. Repeat this process until all have been cooked. Discard any water that may have accumulated around the cooling potatoes. Set aside.

3. In a small mixing bowl, whisk together the lemon juice, mustard, and salt. Stir in the olive oil a little at time. Set aside.

4. To serve, add the defrosted broccoli and the eggs to the cooled potatoes. Stir gently. Pour the dressing over the vegetables, and toss until everything is well coated. Sprinkle the parsley over the salad. Serve at room temperature.

Serves 4

green goddess fruit salad

a refreshing combination of fresh fruit. Make the dressing ahead of time so that it will be well chilled.

Dressing:
½ cup sugar
½ cup water
Juice of 1 lime or
  lemon, or 2 table-
  spoons fruit
  liqueur
Grated peel of 1 lime
  or lemon

Salad:
1 ripe honeydew
  melon, halved,
  seeds removed
3 kiwi fruit, peeled
2 Granny Smith or
  other tart green
  apples, cored
2 ripe green pears,
  cored
½ pound seedless
  green grapes, well
  washed

1. Place the sugar and water in your hot pot and turn the temperature setting to medium. The sugar will begin to dissolve; bring the syrup to a boil and cook it for 5 minutes without stirring. Unplug the hot pot and allow the syrup to cool. Stir in the lime or lemon juice or the liqueur, and the lime or lemon peel. Transfer the syrup to a bowl; cover with plastic wrap and chill.

2. If you have one, use a melon baller to scoop out the flesh of the melon; or cut the melon halves into more manageable pieces, remove the rind, and cut the flesh into bite-size cubes. Place the melon balls or cubes in a large mixing bowl. Set aside.

3. Cut the kiwi fruit into ¼″ slices and then cut each slice in half. Add the kiwi to the melon.

4. Cut the apples and pears into bite-size pieces (do not peel), and add them to the melon and kiwi. Add the green grapes and toss gently.

5. Drizzle the chilled dressing over the salad and toss gently.

Serves 2 to 3

zucchini marinara

a perfect vegetable accompaniment for any meal. Italian seasoning, a blend mostly of oregano and basil, is available in the spice section of the supermarket.

3 small zucchini, washed, ends trimmed, and thinly sliced
½ small onion, finely chopped
½ cup grated Parmesan cheese
1 teaspoon mixed Italian herbs
¾ cup bottled pizza sauce
4 ounces grated mozzarella cheese

1. Preheat your toaster oven to 375° F.

2. Arrange the zucchini slices and chopped onion in an aluminum foil baking pan. Sprinkle the Parmesan cheese and herbs over the vegetables.

3. Pour the pizza sauce over the Parmesan cheese, and cover the pan with aluminum foil. Place the pan in the toaster oven, and bake 40 minutes. Remove the pan from the oven, uncover, and sprinkle the mozzarella cheese over the casserole.

4. Return the pan to the oven and continue baking for approximately 5 minutes, or until the cheese is melted. Switch the toaster oven setting to broil, and broil until the cheese turns golden brown.

5. Remove the zucchini from the oven and serve immediately.

Serves 4

oriental celery

this Oriental-style celery dish is nice to serve with beef fondue or meat loaf for a unique touch.

4 cups finely chopped celery
14- or 17-ounce can water chestnuts, drained and sliced
4-ounce jar pimentos, drained and sliced
10¾-ounce can cream of chicken soup
3 tablespoons soy sauce
½ cup seasoned bread crumbs
3 tablespoons butter, cut into small pieces

1. Preheat the toaster oven to 350° F.

2. Cook the celery, in batches, in rapidly boiling water in your hot pot for 8 minutes or until tender. Transfer the cooked, drained celery to a greased aluminum foil baking pan.

3. Add the rest of the ingredients, in the order given, to the celery. Do not stir; just make layers. Dot the top with the pieces of butter.

4. Place the pan in the toaster oven and bake for 30 minutes. Serve immediately.

Serves 4

desserts

Is your sweet tooth aching for something more than a slice of stale cafeteria carrot cake or a vending machine candy bar? Is the "care" package from home overdue by at least two weeks? Have you been dieting for ages and are ready, now, for a binge? Or maybe you're in search of the perfect finale for your next dinner party. If so, this chapter is for you.

Give your ice cream shop a break. Ice cream goes down so quickly, leaves you still hungry for more, and it can't be stored in our miniature dorm-room freezer compartments. So why not blow the calories on something you can sink your teeth into? Besides, making it yourself is half the fun and you'll have a new appreciation for what you're eating.

By the way, desserts lend themselves especially well

to giving. Whether it's repaying a special friend, a Christmas or other holiday gift, a birthday present for the person who has everything, a hostess present, or merely a token of friendship, you're bound to score high.

I'll always remember how nice it was when on Valentine's Day a friend, who despite my influence was not much of a campus cook, produced a box of homemade chocolate-covered strawberries (my favorite). I was so impressed that I asked for the recipe, and I have included it here.

chocolate-covered strawberries

even though fresh strawberries may be difficult to find in February in time for Valentine's Day, try this elegant confection and you're bound to score points! Do not wash the strawberries before using them unless they are really dirty, because the water keeps the chocolate from sticking. If you really must wash them, pat the strawberries dry with paper towels before dipping.

8 ounces milk chocolate squares
8 ounces semi-sweet chocolate squares
20 ripe strawberries with stems, any bruises removed

1. Melt the chocolates together over low heat in your hot pot. Stir the chocolate continually so that it does not burn.

2. Near the hot pot spread wax paper on which to cool the strawberries once they have been dipped.

3. When the chocolate has completely

(recipe continued on next page)

melted, you may begin dipping the berries. You want to cover as much of the red part of the berry as possible, leaving only the green stem showing. Place the dipped berries on the wax paper and allow the chocolate to set. Serve them immediately or wrap them up as a gift. They should be kept in the refrigerator.

Makes 20

cinnamon-chocolate cake

Certainly you have had chocolate cake in the past, but never so delicious with so little work and so little cleanup! This comes from a very special source and is guaranteed to be a success. It's perfect for a birthday celebration, or a picnic.

½ cup sugar
¾ cup all-purpose flour
3 tablespoons unsweetened cocoa
½ teaspoon baking soda
1 teaspoon vanilla extract
¼ cup vegetable oil
½ cup water
1 teaspoon ground cinnamon
1 to 2 tablespoons powdered sugar

1. Preheat your toaster oven to 375° F.

2. Measure all the ingredients except the powdered sugar directly into an ungreased aluminum foil baking pan. Using the baking pan as a mixing bowl, mix the ingredients together with a fork until the batter is smooth and well blended.

3. Place the pan in the toaster oven and bake for 20 to 25 minutes, or until the center is puffed and the sides pull away from the pan. Remove the cake from the toaster oven and allow it to cool thoroughly before sprinkling generously with

powdered sugar. Add an extra
of cinnamon on top if you're
adventurous.

Serves 4 to 8

vanilla pudding cookies

the pudding makes the cookies rich, the
Bisquick makes them easy. You could use chocolate- or lemon-
flavored pudding mix instead of vanilla. If you do, omit the cinnamon
and roll them in sugar only.

½ cup sugar
1 teaspoon ground
  cinnamon
1 cup Bisquick (or
  1 premeasured
  Bisquick packet)
1 package vanilla
  instant pudding
  mix
1 egg
¼ cup salad oil, or
  4 tablespoons
  (½ stick) soft or
  melted butter

1. Preheat the toaster oven to 350° F.

2. In a small bowl, combine the sugar and
cinnamon until thoroughly blended. Set
aside.

3. Mix the Bisquick, pudding mix, egg,
and oil in a bowl until blended. The dough
will be very dense.

4. Form the dough into small balls
approximately 1″ in diameter and roll them
in the bowl of cinnamon sugar. Then
arrange the balls on an aluminum foil
baking sheet, keeping them 2″ apart. Bake
for 12 minutes, or until they just start to
turn brown. Remove the cookies from the
oven and transfer them to a plate to cool.

Makes 24

chocolate/ peanut butter no-bakes

friends you didn't know you had will be dropping by your room once you've made these cookies. The cooking is done in the hot pot, not in the toaster oven, so they couldn't be easier or quicker to make.

2 tablespoons butter
1½ tablespoons
    unsweetened cocoa
¼ cup milk
1 cup sugar
½ cup peanut butter
    (crunchy or
    smooth)
1½ cups uncooked
    oatmeal
1 teaspoon vanilla
    extract
Pinch of salt

1. Line your tabletop with sheets of wax paper. These will serve as "cookie sheets" later.

2. Place the butter, cocoa, milk, and sugar in your hot pot. Bring the mixture to a boil and then unplug the hot pot.

3. Add the peanut butter, oatmeal, vanilla, and salt to the hot chocolate mixture. Stir until everything is well combined.

4. Drop the mixture by the teaspoonful onto the wax paper. As the mixture cools, it becomes hard, so you will have to work quickly.

5. Allow the cookies to set for 30 minutes before transferring them to a plate or to an airtight container for storage.

Makes 36

mississippi mud

try this recipe, from a friend at the University of Chicago, when you're on a chocolate binge. In some parts of the country, this rich snack is called Rocky Road. Neither name does justice to this calorie-laden concoction!

Batter:
1/3 cup vegetable oil
*2/3 cup plus 1 table-
   spoon sugar*
*2/3 cup self-rising
   flour*
*2 tablespoons
   unsweetened cocoa*
1 egg
*1 1/2 teaspoons
   vanilla extract*

Filling:
*2 cups mini marsh-
   mallows*

Icing:
*5 tablespoons butter,
   well softened*
*1/3 cup unsweetened
   cocoa*
*3/4 cup + 1 table-
   spoon powdered
   sugar*
2 tablespoons milk
*1/2 cup chopped nuts
   (optional)*

1. Preheat the toaster oven to 300° F.

2. In a medium-size bowl, mix all the batter ingredients together until well combined. Pour the batter into an aluminum foil baking pan. Bake for 30 minutes.

3. Remove the cake from the toaster oven and sprinkle the mini marshmallows over the top.

4. Return the pan to the toaster oven and continue baking, at the same temperature, for 10 minutes, or until the marshmallows are soft and starting to melt.

5. While the cake is baking, combine all the icing ingredients except the nuts in a bowl. Beat the mixture with a whisk or wooden spoon until all the lumps are gone. Add the chopped nuts if you're using them. Set aside.

6. Remove the cake from the oven and allow it to cool for 10 minutes. Spread the icing over the marshmallows while the cake is still warm. Allow the cake to cool completely before cutting it into squares.

Serves 4 to 8

seven-layer bars

So easy and so rich and wonderful. This childhood favorite lends itself well to the dorm-room kitchen.

*4 tablespoons
  (½ stick) butter*
*¾ cup graham
  cracker crumbs*
½ cup coconut flakes
*½ cup or 6-ounce
  package semi-
  sweet chocolate
  chips*
*½ cup butterscotch
  chips*
*½ cup chopped
  unsalted nuts
  (optional)*
*7-ounce can sweet-
  ened condensed
  milk*

1. Preheat the toaster oven to 350° F.

2. Place the butter in an aluminum foil baking pan. Melt the butter in the toaster oven. Watch closely, and remove the pan from the oven as soon as the butter has melted. Do not turn the oven off.

3. Arrange the other ingredients, in layers, in the order given, on top of the melted butter, pouring the milk over the top.

4. Place the pan in the toaster oven and bake for 30 minutes. Allow the cookie mixture to cool at least 15 minutes before cutting it into squares. Usually it is hard to wait that long!

Serves 4 to 8

lemon squares

When you're saturated with chocolate, try this recipe as a delicious change for your sweet tooth. So quick and easy, it's perfect for an unexpected occasion.

8 tablespoons (1 stick) butter, softened
1 cup plus 2 tablespoons all-purpose flour
¼ cup powdered sugar
2 eggs, beaten well
1 cup sugar
Juice and grated peel of 1 lemon

1. Preheat the toaster oven to 350° F.

2. Combine the butter, 1 cup flour, and the powdered sugar together in a small mixing bowl. The mixture will be dry and crumbly.

3. Press this crumbly mixture into the bottom of an aluminum foil baking pan to form a crust. Use a spoon to pack it down. Bake it in the toaster oven for 15 minutes, making sure that the crust does not get brown.

4. While the crust is baking, combine the beaten eggs, sugar, 2 tablespoons flour, lemon juice, and lemon peel. (You can use the same bowl you used for the crust— there is no need to wash it out.) Mix well and set aside.

5. Pour the lemon mixture onto the baked crust. Return the pan to the oven and continue baking at the same temperature for an additional 20 to 25 minutes. Remove the pan from the toaster oven and allow it to cool. Cut into squares.

Serves 4 to 8

glazed bananas

This is a very sweet dessert—perfect with coffee after a light dinner. You can prepare the toasted almonds ahead of time in the toaster oven; bake slivered almonds on a sheet of foil at 350° F for 5 minutes, until lightly toasted.

*4 bananas, not too
  ripe
2 tablespoons butter,
  cut into small
  pieces
1 recipe (1 cup)
  Orange Syrup
  (see page 37)
¼ cup slivered
  toasted almonds
  (optional)
½ cup heavy cream
  (optional)*

1. Preheat the toaster oven to 350° F.

2. Peel the bananas and slice them lengthwise. Place them in an aluminum foil baking pan.

3. Dot the bananas with the pieces of butter. Then pour the Orange Syrup over the bananas and butter.

4. Place the pan in the toaster oven just as you sit down to eat; it will take 15 minutes to cook. Baste once or twice, spooning the syrup over the bananas. Bake until soft, but not to the point where they fall apart.

5. Serve warm, with a topping of toasted almonds and/or heavy cream.

Note: If you are using leftover Orange Syrup and don't have quite 1 cup, add brown sugar and orange juice in a 2 to 1 ratio to make up the difference.

Serves 4

chocolate fondue

Create the same friendly atmosphere over dessert as you did with the beef fondue! Have all of your "dipping fixings" cut into bite-size pieces. Sprinkle your fruits with a little lemon juice to prevent them from turning brown.

1 pound milk chocolate bars: Hershey, Cadbury, or your favorite brand
4-ounce dark chocolate bar
¾ cup light cream or evaporated milk
1 tablespoon vanilla extract, or 3 to 4 tablespoons Kahlua or other liqueur

1. Break the candy bars into pieces and place the pieces in your hot pot on a low temperature setting.

2. Add the cream or milk. Stir constantly until the chocolate is melted and the mixture is smooth.

3. Add the vanilla or liqueur just before serving. Serve the fondue right from the hot pot, which should still be plugged in so you can keep the chocolate warm.

There are endless possibilities for dipping into a Chocolate Fondue. Here are a few suggestions:
- Marshmallows
- Ladyfingers
- Pound cake or angel-food cake
- Strawberries, destemmed
- Pineapple chunks
- Mandarin orange slices
- Banana slices
- Apple or peach or pear slices
- Sweet cherries, pitted
- Seedless green grapes

Serves 6

instant gingersnap cake

This no-bake recipe brings together unique ingredients for a surprisingly delightful taste sensation. The whipped cream softens the gingersnaps so that you can actually slice it like a regular cake—and it looks so elegant too.

2 cups or more heavy or whipping cream (see Note)
1 heaping tablespoon powdered sugar
1 teaspoon vanilla extract
11-ounce can mandarin orange slices
½ cup sherry
30 gingersnap cookies

1. If you have access to an electric beater, make real whipped cream: Pour the cream into a medium-size bowl, add the powdered sugar and vanilla, and beat until it forms stiff peaks. Set aside.

2. Drain the mandarin oranges well, reserving 3 tablespoons of the syrup in which they were packed. Place this syrup in a small bowl, add the sherry, and stir. Set this aside.

3. Select 12 orange segments and set these aside for later use as a garnish.

4. Set up an assembly line in the following order: gingersnaps, sherry-syrup mixture, whipped cream, orange segments, and your serving plate. Begin by dipping a gingersnap into the sherry for about 3 seconds per side—no longer or it will start to disintegrate. Remove the cookie from the sherry and spread a small amount of whipped cream on both sides of the cookie. Place the gingersnap upright, vertically, on

the plate and prop it up with a mandarin orange slice. The whipped cream should "adhere" the orange to the cookie, and although it may seem wobbly at first, once you get going the cake will start to take shape. Continue this process, sandwiching the oranges in between cream-laden cookies, and arrange them in a ring, 6″ to 8″ in diameter, on the plate.

5. Don't panic if your ring looks a little messy, because you are going to frost the entire thing with the remaining whipped cream. Depending upon how much you used between layers and the size of the ring, you may need more whipped cream for this next step. Don't be skimpy here! Use a dull knife or a rubber spatula to spread the whipped cream over the top and sides of the cake. With a moistened paper towel, carefully wipe any whipped cream or gingersnap residue from the edge of the plate.

6. Arrange the reserved orange segments on top of the whipped-cream-frosted cake. Cover the cake loosely with plastic wrap, being careful not to disturb the whipped cream. Allow the cake to sit in the refrigerator for at least 2, but not more than 4 hours before serving it.

Note: Or substitute whipped topping for the flavored whipped cream.

Serves 4

apple crisp

There are many variations of this traditional favorite, this one being particularly easy and adaptable. You can use any kind of apple for this recipe, but for the best flavor I recommend a tart cooking apple such as Granny Smith or McIntosh. (In a pinch, use a 25-ounce jar of applesauce.) Serve this warm, plain or with whipped cream, Cool Whip, or Cheddar cheese.

4 large apples, cored and sliced thin (peeling optional)
¼ cup chopped unsalted nuts (optional)
¼ cup raisins (optional)
8 tablespoons (1 stick) butter
½ cup self-rising flour or Bisquick baking mix
¾ cup quick-cooking oatmeal
¾ cup firmly packed brown sugar
1 teaspoon ground cinnamon

1. Preheat the toaster oven to 350° F.

2. Grease an aluminum foil baking pan well. Arrange the sliced apples in the bottom of the pan, and add the nuts and/or raisins on top. Set it aside.

3. Melt the butter in your hot pot on a medium temperature setting. Unplug the hot pot as soon as the butter is completely melted. Add the flour, oatmeal, brown sugar, and cinnamon to the melted butter. Stir until the mixture becomes crumbly.

4. Sprinkle this mixture over the apples. Place the pan in the toaster oven and bake 40 minutes.

Serves 4 to 6

drinks

drinks, both alcoholic and non, are crucial to the way most college students entertain. Everyone has their own secret formulas for favorites, and almost everyone knows how to concoct the old classics—bloody marys, daiquiris, and so on. Try some of the recipes in this chapter for a break from the routine—you'll find them a refreshing change.

While some of these drink recipes contain alcohol, they are also delicious as nonalcoholic beverages. I encourage you to abide by the standing rules of your campus and the state laws as to the use of alcohol.

Let your imagination run wild when making drinks, and try

some unusual (or unlikely) combinations. Such as:

- Combine equal parts of iced tea and ginger ale (or beer) over ice.

- Combine strawberries (fresh or partially thawed frozen ones), fruit-flavored yogurt (or ice cream), and ginger ale in the blender until smooth.

- If you have access to a freezer, try adding a scoop of orange sherbet to your orange juice in the morning. This makes an impressive addition to any brunch.

- Combine lime sherbet and ginger ale (or champagne) in the blender. Garnish with fresh strawberries or blueberries for a cooling and colorful treat.

friendship tea

This recipe makes a great gift. Find an interesting jar or container, tie a ribbon around the outside, and be sure to include a copy of the recipe.

1 envelope lemonade mix
9-ounce jar Tang
1 cup sugar
1 cup presweetened iced tea mix with lemon
1 teaspoon ground cinnamon
1 teaspoon ground cloves

1. Mix all the ingredients together in a bowl. Transfer to an airtight container or jar for storage.

2. To serve: add 1 cup boiling water to 1 to 2 heaping teaspoons of the tea mixture in a mug.

Makes 25 to 30 cups

frozen fruit frappe

The possible combinations of ingredients for this frozen fruit drink are unlimited. It is nutritious, refreshing, low in calories, and substantial enough for a meal. This is also a super way to use up fruit which is a little on the ripe side, or to finish off some bottles of juice or odds and ends you may have in the refrigerator. Add some yogurt, plain or your favorite flavor, to the drink for an interesting variation. But do make sure that you buy frozen berries without sugar or heavy syrup. The syrupy ones are mushy and messy and cannot easily be separated for small portions.

*½ cup fruit juice
(orange, apple,
cranberry, or
white grape juice)
1 small banana,
peeled
1 apple, pear, or
peach, washed and
cored (peeling
optional)
10 to 12 frozen straw-
berries or other
berry, still frozen
(about 1 cup)
Ice cubes, partially
crushed if necessary*

Place all of the ingredients into the blender and blend until smooth.

Serves 1

banana-yogurt milkshake

this is a nutritious and refreshing drink which could substitute as a meal when you're on the run.

---

*1 just-ripe banana,
    peeled*
*½ cup plain,
    vanilla, or banana
    yogurt*
½ cup milk
*10 ice cubes, partially
    crushed (optional)*

1. Place all the ingredients, except for the ice cubes, into the blender bowl. Blend until the drink is thoroughly combined and the banana is puréed.

2. If you'd like the drink to be slushy, add ice cubes, and continue blending until the ice is crushed and has become part of the drink.

Serves 1

cran cooler

this frothy and delicious beverage is wonderful served as a cool and refreshing drink in the summertime.

---

*1 envelope tropical
    punch Kool-Aid
    (see Note)*
¼ cup sugar
½ cup orange juice
*2 cups cranberry
    juice*
*20 ice cubes, partially
    crushed if neces-
    sary*

Place all the ingredients except the ice cubes in the blender. Add a few ice cubes at a time, blending after each addition. Blend until all the ice is crushed and the mixture is frothy. Serve immediately.

Note: If you use diet Kool-Aid, omit the ¼ cup sugar.

Serves 2

sangria

This is a light and refreshing wine and fruit punch—my own adaptation of a recipe that originated in Spain. It is an inexpensive drink and goes a long way. It is also a great way to use up an opened bottle of red wine; any sort of red wine will do, from a burgundy to a sweet Lambrusco.

4 cups red wine
½ cup Tang
1 envelope sweetened lemonade mix
¼ cup fruit liqueur, such as Grand Marnier or apricot brandy (optional)
16-ounce bottle 7-Up or Sprite
17-ounce can fruit cocktail, packed in heavy syrup (see Note)
1 medium orange, unpeeled, cut into thin slices

Combine all the ingredients except the fruit cocktail and the orange slices in a large bowl or pitcher. Once the drink mixes have dissolved, add the fruit cocktail along with its syrup. Float the orange slices on top. Serve the sangria over ice.

Note: You can substitute a can of crushed pineapple or sliced peaches for the fruit cocktail.

Serves 6

mimosas

this is an elegant starter for a special brunch. It is important that all the ingredients are very cold before you begin to prepare the mimosas. You need not buy an expensive variety of champagne, since the orange juice disguises it somewhat.

Ice, crushed if
  possible
1 quart orange juice
1 bottle champagne
Few tablespoons
  Triple Sec, Grand
  Marnier, or
  Cointreau
  (optional)
1 orange, sliced, for
  garnish

1. Fill a tall glass or large wine goblet one-third of the way with ice. Pour in some orange juice until a little less than half full, and then an equal amount of champagne. It is important to pour in the orange juice first, so the drink does not lose its bubbles!

2. Lace the drink with about a teaspoonful of liqueur, if you are using it, and garnish with an orange slice. Serve immediately.

Serves 6 to 8

texas tea

this cool and uniquely refreshing drink will be as big a hit on your campus as it is at Duke. If you happen to have access to a large freezer, the recipe can easily be doubled and frozen in a large airtight container. It's super to serve at parties. Another way to enjoy Texas Tea is as a topping for a fruit salad for a snappy brunch: have your fruit cut up and arranged in individual bowls (a combination of bananas, strawberries, apples, etc.), and just before serving, place one or two of the slush cubes on top, allowing them to melt down into the fruit.

3½ cups water
2 mint tea bags
6-ounce can frozen
  orange juice
  concentrate
6-ounce can frozen
  lemonade concen-
  trate
½ cup sugar
1 cup vodka
6-pack ginger ale,
  diet or regular
1 orange, unpeeled,
  thinly sliced
Mint leaves
  (optional)

1. Bring the water to a boil in your hot pot. Unplug the hot pot and steep the tea bags in the water for about 5 minutes.

2. Pour the mint tea into a large bowl, discarding the tea bags. Add the orange juice and lemonade concentrates, sugar, and vodka. Mix this well until the sugar is dissolved.

3. Pour the liquid into ice cube trays and place the trays in the freezer. The cubes will never become completely frozen because of the alcohol content. Don't worry, all you want is slush.

4. To serve: Place 4 to 5 of the slush cubes into a glass, and fill with ginger ale. The proportion should be ⅔ slush to ⅓ ginger ale. Garnish with a fresh orange slice and, if available, fresh mint leaves.

Serves 8 to 10

hot buttered rum

Mix these few easy ingredients together and keep it in the refrigerator—guaranteed to warm you to the bones in the depths of winter.

8 tablespoons
(1 stick) butter,
softened
2 cups firmly packed
brown sugar
¼ teaspoon ground
cinnamon
¼ teaspoon ground
nutmeg
¼ teaspoon ground
cloves
1 quart dark rum
20 cinnamon sticks

1. Beat the butter and sugar together with a wooden spoon until well incorporated and light and fluffy. Add the spices and beat well. Cover with plastic wrap and refrigerate.

2. To serve: place 1 heaping tablespoon of the spiced butter mixture in a mug. Add 1½ ounces dark rum, and fill the mug with boiling water. Stir with a cinnamon stick.

Serves 20

index